WINE
NO-NONSENSE
GUIDE

WINE NO-NONSENSE GUIDE

FIONA BECKETT

Good Books

IN ASSOCIATION WITH

VICTORIA WINE

For Trevor, who introduced me to the pleasure of good wine

Published in assocation with The Victoria Wine Company
by Good Books (GB Publications Limited)
Lagard Farm, Whitley, Nr Melksham, Wilts SN12 8RL

A CIP catalogue record for this book is available
from the British Library.

ISBN 0 946555 36 2

Designed by Design/Section, Frome
Illustrations by Roy Avis, Blue Chip
Printed and bound in England by Cox & Wyman, Reading

For further information, contact:
The Victoria Wine Company,
Brook House, Chertsey Road, Woking, Surrey GU21 5BE
(Tel: 0483 715066)

Contents

Foreword

Turning the age-old maxim on its head, a little knowledge can be a valuable thing - *when it comes to wine*.

What we've described here as 'no-nonsense' means simply *not* telling you what you will never need to know about wine. You can still swirl, spit and impress with the best of them, safe in the knowledge that understanding the important basics is all you need to enjoy the world of wine to the full.

But if you want to ask for advice, we can still help. Fifteen hundred Victoria Wine branches throughout the UK offer an excellent wine range - from everyday favourites to dusty rarities - and you'll never need lose your bottle if you want some help making a choice. Whether you read a shelf label or talk to one of our staff, we'll tell you everything about a wine in clean, straightforward language - and leave the appreciation to you.

We hope the *No Nonsense Wine Guide* will give you a lasting taste of the enjoyment, and the fun, of wine.

Your good health!

The Victoria Wine Company
November 1994

Introduction

What you *don't* need to know about wine

In the past, many people have been put off wine by the wine trade itself. Pinstripe–suited wine merchants and snooty wine waiters seemed to delight in shrouding the subject with as much mystique as possible – rambling on about vintages, peppering their conversation with obscure French terms like *grand cru* and *assemblage*, wincing when you pronounced the name of a wine the wrong way. Wine was either expensive and French, cheap and Spanish, or sweet and German, and that was about it.

Since then there has been a total revolution. Wine now comes from all over the world, from Australia to Argentina. You can buy it bone crisp and dry or crammed full of tropical fruit flavours, fresh and young or rich and velvety; cheap, moderately priced or expensive. You can buy it straight off the shelf in every kind of shop from the corner shop to the supermarket. The result is that we've all become a continental-style nation of wine drinkers.

But some of the mystique still lingers on. Although shop assistants (and even wine waiters) are friendly, although labels on bottles are informative, we're still nervous about experimenting for fear of making a mistake. At the back of this is the idea that to buy a good bottle of wine you need to be an expert. In fact, nothing could be further from the truth.

Three things you *don't* need to know about wine

You don't need to worry about vintages. Vintages are much less important than they used to be because wines are now made for drinking straightaway rather than keeping for years.

You don't need to remember the names of châteaux. If you want to, of course, you can. But don't worry if you can't tell one Bordeaux wine from another. These days the easiest way to remember wines is by the grape variety they are made from.

You don't need to know how wine is made. Lots of wine books go into great detail about how wines are produced. This one doesn't. It's what it tastes like that's important.

What you *do* need to know

What we all need to be able to do is to walk into a wine shop, recognise the wines on the shelf, and be able to pick the right wine for the right occasion. And that's what this book is all about.

You can read as little or as much of it as you want. If you read the first section you'll have enough basic knowledge to get by. Move on to Part II and you'll learn how to identify the style of wine you like. Part III will tell you when it is and isn't worth buying Champagne and introduce you to two great underrated wines – sherry and dessert wines. Part IV explains how wine and food go together so you can always work out how to pick the right wine with what you're eating, and Part V deals with wines for special occasions and celebrations. If you want to know what wine to serve for a party or a romantic dinner for two, this is where to look.

A word to women

This book is for women too. That should go without saying but often we leave it to the men (or they automatically take it on themselves) to buy the wine. Don't let them have all the fun.

Much of the wine that appears on the shelves is actually selected by women, so there's no reason why you shouldn't be the one who's picking the bottles in your household.

Taste, taste, taste

Finally, the best way to learn is by tasting. The more different kinds of wine you try, the more knowledgeable you will be. It's as simple as that.

PART I

Back To Basics

CHAPTER 1

Five Words You Need to Know to be a Wine Buff

Let's face it, it's not easy walking into a wine shop. You get through the door and there are 200-odd bottles staring you in the face. You don't know what they taste like or whether they'll go with what you're eating. The names on the labels all look double-dutch. The temptation is either to clutch gratefully at any bottle you recognise or dither helplessly for ten minutes and then sneak out while the sales assistant isn't looking.

It doesn't have to be like that. Wine isn't the great mystery it's sometimes made out to be. In fact, there are just five words you need to know to become a wine buff.

Instead of the complicated names you used to find on bottles – Château this and Domaine that – today many bottles carry just a single word: the name of the grape from which the wine was made. Remember the name, get acquainted with what the wine tastes like, and picking a bottle becomes a breeze.

The five most common names you'll come across are Chardonnay and Sauvignon (both white wines) and Cabernet, Merlot and Shiraz (all reds).

Chardonnay

Chardonnay (pronounced *shar-don-nay*) is one of the world's great white grapes which goes to make some of the world's most expensive and sought-after wines. Chablis is Chardonnay, the fabulous Puligny-Montrachet is Chardonnay. Most Champagne contains Chardonnay.

But nowadays everyone's leaping on the Chardonnay bandwagon.

You can buy Australian Chardonnay, Californian Chardonnay, South African Chardonnay, Hungarian Chardonnay – you name a country that grows wine, it grows Chardonnay.

Why is it so popular? Because it can be made so many different ways. It can be light, melony and refreshing. It can have the rich, nutty taste of vanilla. It can be ripe, tropical and fruity. Technically it's a dry wine, but it doesn't taste dry. It is the ultimately adaptable wine which goes with almost any kind of food. You can drink it winter or summer, with salmon or steak. Chardonnay is a boon.

Good value Chardonnay comes from: Australia, South Africa, Hungary and the South West of France – the strangely named Pays d'Oc.

Sauvignon
(*So-vee-nyong*)

Sauvignon or Sauvignon Blanc, as it's sometimes called, has a clean, fresh, sharp taste – the kind you'll go for if you like fresh lemon juice, Granny Smith apples or gooseberries (just try sniffing a glass and you'll see what I mean). It's best known as the grape that goes into the classic wines of the Loire region of France like Sancerre, but it also works particularly well in New Zealand where its gorgeous, green gooseberryish character really comes to the fore.

Sauvignon makes lovely summer drinking and is the perfect partner for salads and grilled fish. It also goes wickedly well with smoked salmon.

Good value Sauvignon comes from: France, New Zealand, Chile, South Africa.

Cabernet Sauvignon
(*Ca-bear-nay so-vee-nyong*)
Cabernet Sauvignon (known in the trade as 'Cab') is an elegant sort

of a grape which makes the kind of wine you bring out for a dinner party or Sunday lunch. Traditionally it has been mainly used in Bordeaux to make claret – what many people consider to be the ultimate red wine. In the hands of New World winemakers, in countries such as Chile, it can be gorgeously rich and fruity, full of the taste of blackcurrants and blackberries. Because it can be a bit severe on its own it is often blended with other grapes such as Merlot and Shiraz (look out for descriptions such as Cabernet/Merlot, Cabernet/Shiraz) to make it softer and fruitier.

Cabernet is the perfect partner for steak, traditional roasts and other meat dishes, but can also work surprisingly well with spicier dishes like a curry (though stick to fruitier Cabernets from countries like Australia and Chile).

Good value Cabernet comes from: Australia, Bulgaria, Chile, France.

Merlot
(Mer-low)

Where Cabernet is big and beefy, Merlot is soft, supple and juicy – the reason why they work so well together in the classic Bordeaux blend. On its own Merlot makes wonderfully ripe, fruity wines which sometimes taste of raspberries, sometimes of plums. If you like a lighter red, go for wines from the most recent vintage – Hungarian Merlots are particularly fresh and zippy.

Merlot's big plus is that you can team it with a wide variety of meat, chicken and cheese dishes. It's one of the few wines that stand up well to a strong tomato flavour, which makes it a good match with pizza and pasta.

Wine buff's tip

While Merlot makes soft, easy drinking wines it is also the grape that goes into one of the most famous and expensive red wines in the world, Château Pétrus. A magnum (equivalent to two bottles) of 1961 Pétrus, for instance, would set you back about £2,500.

Good value Merlot comes from: Hungary, Italy, Chile, the South West of France (the Pays d'Oc).

Shiraz

(She-raz)

Known as Syrah (*See-ra*) in France, Shiraz in Australia and other
newer wine-producing countries, the Shiraz grape makes a big, beefy,
spicy wine – a real red wine-drinkers' red. In the South of
France it is the grape used to make many
of the very famous (and expensive)
Rhône wines such as Côte-Rôtie and
Hermitage, which are fabulously rich
and opulent. In the hands of the
Aussies it's just so wonderfully big,
bright and brash, it's the perfect
wine for a barbie.

**Good value Shiraz (Syrah)
comes from**: Australia and France.

There. That wasn't so painful, was it? Five minutes reading and
you can now recognise at least a quarter of the wines you're likely to
find on a wine shop shelf.

CHAPTER 2

A Quick Whizz Round the World

As we've already established, you don't need to know a lot about where wine comes from but it helps to know where you can get good value. The wine map's changed enormously in the last twenty years or so and there is a whole lot of new wine-producing countries on the scene that you wouldn't have dreamt of buying from before.

These newer countries - Australia, California, Chile, New Zealand and South Africa - are called the New World. The traditional wine-producing countries of France, Germany, Italy, Spain, Portugal and Eastern Europe are called the Old World. Just five years ago there used to be quite a difference: New World wines were far more upfront and fruity. But even in so-called Old World countries like France there are up-and-coming areas like the Languedoc which are making exciting, New World-style wines which are terrific value for money.

Here's what you need to know to get by (you can find out more about individual wines in Chapter 7):

Old World Wines

France

France is still the world's greatest wine-producing nation, the source of the world's most famous wines - Bordeaux, Burgundy, and Champagne. After resting on its laurels for years, often asking too much for dull wines, it has now responded to competition from the

New World with a torrent of excellent wine, much of which comes from lesser known areas.

There are six important wine-growing regions:

Bordeaux

Bordeaux is huge. It produces a staggering six million bottles a year and has five times as many vineyards as its main rival Burgundy. Most famous for its reds, it also produces light elegant whites, and succulently sweet dessert wines. The reds are sometimes referred to as claret and include the Cabernet and Merlot grapes. They tend to be rich, smooth, heavy wines, better for drinking with food than on their own.

Burgundy

Both white and red Burgundy is famous – and easier to remember than other regions because the whites are made from Chardonnay, and the reds from the Pinot Noir grape (see Chapter 6). They tend to be (and are better when they are) expensive. The best known white is Chablis. Just to the south of the Burgundy region is Beaujolais, which is famous for its light, fruity reds.

Champagne

Still the world's greatest sparkling wine though nowadays there are many good imitators (see Chapter 9). The most surprising thing is how far north Champagne is grown: in the northeast of France on a level with Paris.

Loire

The Loire valley in the northwest of France is famous for its white wines: bone-dry Muscadet and elegant, expensive wines made from the Sauvignon grape like Sancerre and Pouilly-Fumé. It is a region that has been overtaken by other areas in the value-for-money stakes but at its rather pricey best makes elegant, crisp wines which are hard to beat.

Rhône

The Rhône Valley in the south of France produces some of the most sumptuous, rich, voluptuous reds around, the best known of which are Hermitage (from the north of the region) and Châteauneuf-du-

Pape (from the south). More affordable is the light, fruity, easy drinking Côtes du Rhône.

Alsace

The great underrated wine region of France which makes some very classy white wines – a bit like a cross between German and French wines (not surprisingly as Alsace is on the German/French border). Alsace is best known for Gewürztraminer, a once-tasted, never-forgotten wine which goes wonderfully with spicy food.

Vin de Pays

The best value in France often comes from humble country wines or *vin de pays* where winemakers don't have to meet strict rules and regulations and can play around with different grapes and go-ahead techniques. (More on these wines in Chapter 7.)

Good French wine buys

Tricky to pick. The great French classics can be unbeatable, but you still come across wines that are trading on their reputation. For value for money, it's hard to beat wines from France's most exciting up-and-coming wine region, the Languedoc, down in the south. Look for wines from the Pays d'Oc, many of which are labelled with their grape variety (it's a source of very good Chardonnay). There are also some stunning reds from the Corbières and Minervois in the same region.

Italy

Italy is the most confusing wine area of the world, with so many different grapes and no big wine regions to get a handle on. The

easiest approach is to remember what Italy is best for: very fresh, clean, dry whites, lovely, rich, vibrant fruity reds and soft, sweetish, low-cost sparklers (Asti Spumante is a good deal better than the rather flavourless Lambrusco). The quality of the wines is much better than it was a few years ago when Italy was churning out dull flabby whites and soft floppy reds.

White wines like Frascati (*Fras-car-tea*) and Soave (*Sue-arvay*) and reds like Chianti (*key-anti*) and Valpolicella (*Val-poly-chella*) have improved out of sight.

Good Italian wine buys

The emerging south of Italy, which is producing exciting, reasonably priced wines, is the region to focus on. Merlot is a grape that has found a natural home in Italy, producing rich, fruity reds - look for Merlot on the label.

Germany

There's a strange contradiction about German wines. The less distinguished ones such as Liebfraumilch are hugely popular, while the really good ones (which are almost all white and made from the Riesling grape) are only bought in tiny quantities.

In fact, German wines have a lot going for them; they're low in alcohol, wonderfully refreshing, good with food and there are also some knockout sweet wines. The big drawback is getting to grips with the names. Three words that are useful to remember are Kabinett (pronounced as it looks – *Cabin-ett*) which is light and fresh, Spätlese (*spate-laser*) which is fuller and richer (and can be dry or off-dry) and Auslese (*Ows-laser*) which is generally quite sweet.

Good German wine buys
Riesling (see more on this grape in Chapter 6).

Spain

Spain is another country with a 'cheap and cheerful' image problem. Actually it produces some very serious reds – the best known of which is Rioja (*ree-och-ar*) – sherry and a great, low-cost sparkler, Cava (see Chapter 9). Along with Eastern Europe it's one of the best sources of bargain drinking.

Good Spanish wine buys
Better to buy by the region than the grape. Look out for low-cost wines from La Mancha, Navarra, Valencia and Valdepeñas (*Val-de-pen-yas*).

Portugal

Best known for port, Portugal isn't generally associated with wine except for the ubiquitous Mateus Rosé and the slightly characterless Vinho Verde. Nowadays it produces some fresh, clean, lemony whites and some terrific, full, gusty reds.

Good Portuguese wine buys
Worth experimenting with some of the very modestly priced reds.

Eastern Europe

Once Eastern Europe just meant Bulgarian cheapies. Now Hungary has taken off with Moldova (part of the former USSR) and Slovakia snapping at its heels. This is a part of the world that has seen huge growth and now provides some of the best value wines on the market, thanks to the arrival on the scene of British and Australian winemakers.

Eastern European wines are easy to buy because they are labelled with the grape variety they are made from. As well as cut price classics like Cabernet Sauvignon, it is now starting to offer wines made from its own exotically named local grape varieties – such as the light, medium-dry white Irsai Oliver, and fresh raspberryish Gamza.

Good Eastern European wine buys
Almost anything under £3 is worth a whirl. Look out specially for Bulgarian Cabernet Sauvignon, Hungarian Sauvignon, Chardonnay and Merlot, and Romanian Pinot Noir.

Other Old World Wines

Austria, Germany's next door neighbour, makes some very good wines but they seldom come our way, apart from the rather dreary Grüner Veltliner.

England used to be treated as a bit of a joke but is now producing some stylish, fresh, crisp whites at an affordable price.

Greece is not a great wine-producing country. Best remembered by holidaymakers for that love-or-hate-it wine Retsina, it is now producing a few fresh lemony whites and full-flavoured reds.

New World Wines

Australia

Australia can do no wrong, in most people's eyes at least. Its wines are wonderfully upfront, vibrant and fruity, and easy to recognise. Whites, reds, sparklers, stickies (as the Aussies call sweet wines), inexpensive or pricey, Australia makes them all.

Good Australian wine buys
Just about everything - most famously Chardonnay and Shiraz.

New Zealand

With its cool, almost European climate New Zealand might not at first seem an obvious wine-growing country. But it has become

famous for its stunning Sauvignon Blancs. It is now making some
good reds too.

Good New Zealand wine buys
Sauvignon Blanc, Cabernet Sauvignon.

California

California is not one of the world's cheapest wine-producing areas,
but round about the £5 mark and over, quality can be very good.
Almost all wines are varietals – that is, made from and named after a
single grape. Look out for California's own grape variety, Zinfandel,
a robust, fruity red.

Good Californian wine buys
Chardonnay, Pinot Noir, Zinfandel.

Chile

The most promising of the South American wine-producing
countries, Chile hasn't quite hit the international jackpot in the same
way as Australia. But it makes marvellous, intense, fruity wines at an
affordable price.

Good Chilean wine buys
Sauvignon, Cabernet Sauvignon and Merlot.

South Africa

During the years of sanctions, the South Africans quietly went on
making wines and are now reaping the benefit. Next to Australia,
they have the broadest selection of styles to offer, some made from
lesser known grapes – Chenin Blanc, Colombard and Pinotage – as
well as Chardonnay, Merlot and Cabernet Sauvignon. South Africa is
a kind of halfway house between the Old and New World – more
upfront than the French, a bit more restrained than the Australians.

Good South African wine buys

Inexpensive fruity whites (Chenin Blanc and Colombard) and rich, plummy red Pinotage. Well-priced Sauvignon, Chardonnay, Cabernet Sauvignon, and Merlot.

Another New World Country To Watch

Argentina (the fifth largest wine producer in the world) used to make very rough and ready wines. Now it is beginning to make some very stylish reds, particularly from the Malbec grape.

CHAPTER 3

Tasting Wine

There's more mystique about tasting wine than almost anything else. First of all there's that great performance you see the wine expert go through – all that swilling, sniffing, slurping and spitting. Then there's the language they use to describe the experience, which ranges from the obscurely technical (acidic, tannic) to comparisons with cigar boxes and sweaty saddles, which doesn't make the wine sound very enticing at all.

All this nonsense tends to obscure the real value of tasting, which is that you begin to pick up more complex smells and flavours in wine which makes the whole experience much more pleasurable and helps you to understand what it means when other people talk or write about wine in a certain way.

How to taste... and drink wine

The point about tasting wine – and you adopt pretty much the same technique when you drink it – is that it's a terrible waste of what should be a nice bottle of wine to gulp it down in one go like a glass of lemonade (and a sure-fire way of getting drunk). Take it slowly and you'll

enjoy the experience a whole lot more.

There are four easy stages:

■ First fill your glass a third full, then take a look at the wine in it. It should be a clear, bright colour (even old wines which tend to be more faded shouldn't appear cloudy).

■ Holding the glass by the stem, swirl it around a couple of times. The point of doing this is to let wine move around and release the bouquet or smell of the wine.

■ Raise it to your nose and sniff it. This should be pretty enjoyable. In almost all cases the wine will taste the same as it smells, so you're getting two bites at the cherry.

■ Raise the glass to your lips and take a small sip. Let it linger a little bit, rolling it around in your mouth before you swallow it.

The point of doing the last stage nice and slow is that you often get two different flavours from a mouthful of wine – what the professionals call the front taste (the immediate sensation you get when the wine hits your mouth) and the back taste (the lingering sensation you are left with after you have swallowed it). The better the wine, the longer the taste lasts.

If you're drinking wine rather than tasting it you don't have to go through the sniffing routine each time, but still don't overfill your glass and don't swig it down.

Do I have to spit it out?

The idea of spitting is pretty disgusting to those who don't have to do it for a living. If you've got fifty wines to taste it's pretty well essential, otherwise you'd end up horizontal. What the professional wine tasters do is to suck the wine noisily through their mouth – to get the air in so they can taste it better – then spit it out (there's a certain macho pride in seeing how far you can do it). Unless you're sampling more than half a dozen wines, don't worry about it.

Corked wine

You can tell pretty quickly once you smell a wine if there's something wrong with it. If it smells like damp, mouldy cellars, it is said to be corked. Wine should also not smell like bad eggs, vinegar or overripe rotting fruit. If you think there's something wrong, bung the cork back in and take it back to the shop you bought it from as soon as you can (it may not be practical to do it the same evening but don't wait a month and then expect to get your money back).

Understanding winespeak

One of the most difficult things about wine is understanding what other people say about it. Once you get beyond white and red, different words can mean different things to different people. Sweet and dry are the most notorious examples.

Most regular wine drinkers would not think of Australian Chardonnay as a particularly dry wine – they would use that word to describe a bone-dry white wine like a Muscadet – but to someone used to drinking Liebfraumilch it probably would seem dry.

Some words also relate to the texture of wine. There are words which mean something to people who taste wine every day of their lives, such as fat, buttery or oily (all, believe it or not, compliments) which are hard to make sense of for a novice wine drinker.

Twenty useful wine words

In fact, you don't need a lot of knowledge to get by. There are twenty words commonly used about wine it may help you to understand.

Acidity
Sounds nasty but is, generally speaking, a compliment. Acidity is what gives wines that mouth-tinglingly juicy feel. Wines made from the Sauvignon grape tend to be high in acidity.

Bouquet
A much used wine word which simply means what a wine smells like. Can also be called the wine's 'nose'.

Clean
Clean seems an odd word to use of wine – you wouldn't exactly expect it to be dirty. In winespeak, it tends to mean a dry, fresh white.

Complex
Means a wine that's got some character rather than having a simple uncomplicated flavour.

Crisp
Generally used of very dry white wine to describe the clean, slightly sharp (though not sour) sensation you get when you drink it.

Flowery/Floral
Not literally flowery. Often used to describe very full fragrant wines, particularly from Germany.

Fruity
The word that's most widely used of wine. Wines can be fruity in all kinds of ways, though funnily enough seldom grapey. Whites can be lemony or gooseberryish (Sauvignon), peachy or melony (both Chardonnay), while reds can be blackcurranty (Cabernet Sauvignon), raspberryish or plummy (Merlot), or they may simply be described as berryish. (Try smelling a glass of New Zealand Sauvignon and a glass of Australian Cabernet Sauvignon and you'll see what I mean.)

Full/Full-bodied
Means the wine is going to be quite strong-tasting (and generally high in alcohol). Most commonly used of reds, though sometimes of New World Chardonnay.

Long/Lingering
Good wines are 'long in the mouth' - that means that the taste lingers on after you have swallowed a mouthful, leaving you with a pleasant rather than a harsh aftertaste.

Oaky
Many wines - both white and red - are put in oak casks to age them. That can lend a distinctive taste to the wine, depending on the age of the wood: old oak literally tastes woody, new oak (which is often used in white wines) intensifies their fruitiness and can give them a vanilla-y, toasty flavour.

Soft
Used more of reds than whites to describe an easy drinking wine without any harsh tannins (see below) or particularly marked acidity. The
terms 'smooth' and 'well-rounded' mean pretty much the same thing.

Spicy
May seem a strange word to describe a wine but it tends to be used
of distinctively aromatic wines such as Gewürztraminer, or strong-
flavoured wines made from the Syrah or Shiraz grape, which are
sometimes also referred to as peppery.

Structure
The structure of a wine is a bit like a story. When you taste it, it
should have a beginning, a middle and an end. Only more expensive
wines do.

Tannic/Tannin
Tannin is a sensation rather than a taste, like the furred-up feeling you
get in your mouth when you drink a strong cup of tea. Many red
wines like claret used to be tannic. Now most are made in a fruitier
style.

Young/Youthful
Generally used of a wine that's 6-12 months old. It can be
complimentary - implying that it's zippy and fresh - or a criticism that
it's still slightly green and stalky.

Most wine words you'll find on a bottle are complimentary. But
you may come across words elsewhere which indicate a wine isn't so
good. Here are five:

Cabbagey
While fruit is a desirable quality in a wine, cabbage certainly isn't.
Any wine that has that slightly sour smell of well-used washing-up
water isn't worth drinking.

Flabby
Wines shouldn't be flabby any more than bodies should. A flabby
wine is a wine that hasn't got enough acidity.

Harsh
A harsh wine is what we used to refer to as plonk, the kind of wine that tastes like paint stripper as it goes down.

Oxydised
Oxydised is a technical term meaning that air has got into the bottle and spoilt the wine. Most noticeable in whites, it can give them a dark yellow colour and a rather stewed, unpleasant taste.

Thin
Not a compliment in wine terms. A watery wine without much fruit.

CHAPTER 4

Buying and Keeping Wine

Most of the wine you will buy will be in bottles. The standard size 75cl (which holds 27fl oz – enough for five or six glasses), though some wines are sold by the litre or in a 37.5cl half bottle (particularl' dessert wines). A few wines are also sold in magnums, which is equivalent to two standard bottles.

You may notice these bottles come in different styles, which nowadays means less than it used to when certain types of wine such as Bordeaux and Burgundy always came in the same shaped bottle. Whites are generally bottled in clear glass, and reds in green, though you may find both in brown.

Wine boxes

Modern technology has made it possible for wine to be kept in large foil pouches inside a cardboard box. To get at the wine you simply pull out the little tap, press it and fill up your glass (or at leas that's the theory – personally I always have an epic struggle to pull the tap out).

The advantage of having a wine box is that you can always have your favourite wine on hand, just pulling off a glass or two when y feel like it. The disadvantage is that that can be pretty boring,

particularly if you live on
your own (a three-litre
box holds the equivalent
of four standard bottles –
that's about 24 glasses).

Although the quality
of wine boxes has
improved enormously
since they were first
introduced at the
beginning of the eighties,
the wine inevitably
deteriorates over time. If
you're unlikely to drink it up within
a fortnight, you'd be better off with a bottle
and some kind of wine-preservation gadget
(see below).

How much should I pay for a bottle?

Two thirds of the wine that is sold in this country is under £3 a
bottle, and nowadays there are some terrific wines on offer at this
price. What you have to remember is that the cheaper the wine, the
higher the proportion of the cost that goes in duties and taxes.
Currently a £2.99 bottle will only contain about 34p worth of grapes,
whereas a bottle that costs £4.99 will contain wine worth 53p.

What you pay is really a matter of horses for courses. For everyday
consumption an inexpensive easy drinking wine is fine. For entertaining
or special occasions it's worth paying a bit more (see Part V).

Reading the label

Having got this far you already know a fair bit about wine, but when
you actually come to buy a bottle you need to check out the label.
Wine labels vary between one country and another but there are
certain things that are common:

■ the amount of wine in the bottle – usually 75cl.

■ the alcoholic strength of the wine – expressed as % vol or volume.
Most wines are between 10 and 13 per cent, which doesn't seem a

Retail price
£4.99

Fixed costs
£1.86
(VAT £0.74
Exise £1.02
Freight £0.10)

Retailer profit
£1.25

Winemaker's
profit £1.05

Dry goods/Prod
costs £0.30

Grapes £0.53

huge variation but can make all the difference between a light and quite heavily alcoholic wine (see Chapter 22).

■ the name of the producer, which is usually tucked away in small print at the bottom.

Most wine bottles today also carry a back label which contains useful information about what the wine tastes like, where it's made, the kind of food you can serve with it and how long you can keep it.

Does the vintage matter?

Wine buffs will tell you that the vintage (that is the year the wine was made) is important – and so it is if you're buying expensive château-bottled claret. But for most of the wines you're likely to buy it's not so critical. Of course wines vary between one year and another depending on the weather during the harvest, but modern wine-making techniques are so sophisticated that winemakers can iron out most of the problems. Some wines, like the popular Australian Jacob's Creek, don't put a year on the bottle precisely because they pride themselves on being able to produce a wine that tastes the same year after year.

Most of the wines you will buy will have been produced in the last couple of years. (It takes 6-9 months on average for a wine to appear on the market so in 1995 you can expect to see 94s and 93s from European countries like France, Spain and Italy, and even some 95s from New World countries like Australia and South Africa, who have their harvest six months earlier.) Buying young wine is more critical with whites than reds: a good rule of thumb is to go for the most recent vintage on the shelf.

Storing wine

Once you get your bottle (or bottles) home you need to find
somewhere to keep it if you're not going to drink it straightaway.
Basically, wine is happiest on its side (the origin of the phrase 'laying
down' a bottle) simply because the wine keeps the cork moist so it
can't dry out and let air into the bottle.

If you're keeping the wine for any length of time you should also
find somewhere that is dark, so the light can't get to the wine, and a
reasonably even temperature (so not in the airing cupboard next to
the hot-water tank). A garage isn't a bad place, particularly if it's built
on to the house, but probably the best hideout is the cupboard under
the stairs.

If you've got more than half a dozen bottles it's worth investing
in a wooden wine rack so they don't get smashed every time
someone wants to get the hoover out.

How long should I keep wine?

Not long at all. The idea that you have to 'lay wine down' for
several years stems from a time when wines were made big, tough
and tannic. Nowadays most wines are made to be drunk within the
year and few wines benefit from being kept for more than six
months.

Once you've opened a bottle there's simply no point in keeping
it for more than a couple of days. There are several impressive-
looking gadgets on the market for keeping a bottle fresh once you've
opened it, the easiest and most inexpensive of which are the
Winesaver (an aerosol can which squirts a layer of inert gas over the
wine to stop the air getting at it) and the Vacu-Vin – a combination
of a rubber stopper and a plastic pump. You simply pump the air out
of the bottle and the wine will keep in reasonable condition for 3-5
days. Whites last less time than reds and should be kept in the fridge.

CHAPTER 5

Serving Wine

Serving wine can be a nerve-racking experience, especially if you're doing it for the first time in front of guests. The easiest thing is to do it out of sight in the kitchen, particularly if you're opening a bottle of Champagne or sparkling wine (see Chapter 9).

Opening a bottle

Part of the problem of getting a bottle open is that corkscrews come in all kinds of shapes and sizes. It's actually worth splashing out on a decent corkscrew that does the hard physical work of yanking the cork out for you. The two simplest and most straightforward ones I've tried (and opening bottles without making a hash of it has never been one of my great strengths) are the Brabantia and the pocket Screwpull, which conveniently also has a cutter to score round the top of the bottle and remove the foil or plastic cap. Both are widely available at under £10.

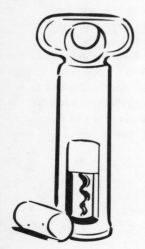 

What if the cork gets stuck in the bottle?

If the cork breaks halfway through pulling it out (which it shouldn't if you're using one of these demon gadgets) there is yet another implement you can buy, with uneven-sided prongs designed to deal with this kind of emergency. If you haven't got one to hand, try inserting the point of the corkscrew from a slightly different angle and try again. If the cork's gone right down you can either ignore it or, if there are little pieces of cork floating around in the bottle, whip the glasses off the table and filter the wine into them with a clean tea strainer.

Decanting wine

Decanting wine (pouring it out of the bottle and into a glass decanter) used to be commonplace when wine was unfiltered and laid down for years and you might otherwise get a mouthful of sediment. With most modern wines it's simply not necessary.

If, however, you're given a particularly serious bottle of claret or have inherited granny's exquisite cut-glass decanter, by all means go ahead. Leave the bottle upright for at least twenty-four hours, then pour it slowly and steadily into the decanter (if you have a light directly behind the bottle you can see any sediment which might be threatening to sneak through). Don't do it too far beforehand: an hour before you're due to drink it is quite enough.

How far ahead should I open wine?

Like decanting, there's a whole lot of folklore about needing to open a bottle well before you drink it. With most modern wines - certainly any light white or red wine - you don't need to bother. However there are big, gutsy red wines like Italian Barolo or some of the southern French reds which benefit from letting the air get to them. By and large, the label on the back of the bottle will advise you.

Serving wine at the right temperature

This is the one thing you do need to get right. The old rule was that you served whites cold and reds at room temperature; but that was in the days before central heating. In fact many reds such as Beaujolais taste pretty good chilled, a nice way of drinking them on a hot summer's day.

Rather better advice nowadays is that if a wine is light, young, sweet or sparkling (and that includes most whites), it's better served cold. If it's full, rich or aged (several years old) – and that includes most reds – it's better at room temperature, though you should still avoid overheating a red wine by leaving it next to a radiator or the cooker. Light reds and full-bodied whites like Australian Chardonnay can be chilled lightly.

The easiest way to chill a wine is to leave it in the fridge for 2-3 hours, depending on how cold your fridge is. (You shouldn't, even with a sweet wine, let it get too cold or you kill the flavour.) If you need to chill wine in a great hurry you can pop a bottle in the freezer compartment for twenty minutes, but it's not really advisable in case you forget it's there and the bottle explodes.

Wine buff's tip

Some of the classiest (and most expensive) glasses in the world are made by an Austrian glassmaker, Georg Riedel, who has a theory that there is a perfect glass for every grape variety. (Sounds crazy but it works.) His ultimate glass is a 37fl oz monster for drinking red Burgundy, which holds over a bottle of wine. Of course you don't fill it that full, so what you get is 4fl oz of wine and 33fl oz of bouquet.

The simplest solution is to buy a natty little jacket for the wine, called Rapid Ice, which you simply keep in the freezer and pop on a bottle when you want to drink it. It is a bit of a struggle to get it on some Champagne bottles, and it takes a bit longer than they say to chill the wine properly (about 10–15 minutes), but it's quicker than anything else. You can also keep a wine cold on the table once you have opened it by popping it into a wine cooler.

Wine glasses

Before you finally get to the point of pouring your wine, a word about wine glasses. Unfortunately the last thing many of us think of when we buy a set of glasses is whether wine will taste any good out of them. We're far more concerned with how pretty they look.

From the wine's point of view, the plainer the glass the better; cut or coloured glass may look flashy but it obscures the wine it's supposed to show off.

In general, big glasses are much better than small ones: it means you can fill them half full (to release the wine's aromas) but still have plenty of wine in your glass. An inwardly curved rim is preferable to the traditional rolled rim of the Paris goblet, which tends to hold the wine back and then release it in a great *whoosh* down your throat.

Keeping glasses clean

Just as important as the shape of a glass is how clean it is. A greasy glass or one that hasn't been properly rinsed can really spoil the taste of a wine. The best way to wash your glasses is as soon as possible after using them, rinse them in the hottest water you can bear and dry them with a clean, soft, dry linen tea towel (also well rinsed or you can pick up the taste of detergent on your glass). Dishwashers are efficient but can scratch good glasses over time.

Pouring wine

Even when you're at home and not in a restaurant it pays to check any wine you serve before pouring it into anyone else's glass. Follow the tasting countdown on page 27, then if there is something wrong with the wine you can open another bottle (a good reason for having one or two spares).

When you pour the wine, remember to fill the glass only halfway so your guests (and you, of course) can enjoy the smell as well as the taste.

PART II

Getting More Confident

CHAPTER 6

Five More Great Grapes

OK, so now you know the basics. You can find your way round a
wine shop. But there are still some interesting bottles lurking there
you may not know about. For a start, there's another five grapes –
three white, two red – you could usefully get to know.

Chenin Blanc
(Sher-nan blong)

Chenin is an unusual grape that makes two contrasting styles of wine,
depending on whether it's made into a dry or sweet wine. In the
New World – countries like Australia and South Africa – it makes a
smooth, well-rounded, soft, creamy wine with ripe melony fruit. But
in the Loire region of France, where it's used to make the great semi-
sweet wine Vouvray (a hugely underrated wine), it can be luscious,
rich, honeyed and lingering.

Dry Chenin is a perfect match for light meat like chicken or veal
in a creamy sauce. Sweeter Chenin like Vouvray drinks deliciously
with a classic French apple tart.

Good value Chenin comes from: South Africa, Australia, France.

Riesling
(Ree-sling)

If you thought all German wine was Liebfraumilch or Hock, think
again. Many of the great German white wines are made from a grape
called Riesling, and they're luscious. The taste is hard to describe; it's
a bit like biting into a very soft, ripe fruit, mouth-wateringly juicy
and sweet without being sugary. In recent years it's been rather
unfashionable but there are signs of it staging a comeback, not least
because the energetic Aussies have been giving it a whirl.

Riesling's great virtue – although it's delicious to drink on its own – is that it's fabulous with food, particularly with slightly spicy, oriental dishes which are tricky to match with other wines. Some of the sweeter German Rieslings which have the words Spätlese or Auslese on the label make perfect pudding wines.

Good value Riesling comes from: Germany, Australia, the Alsace region of France.

Sémillon
(Se-mee-yong)

Sémillon is a bit of a shrinking violet, seldom seen on its own. But it's a crucial grape in the very famous white wines of Bordeaux, where it's blended with Sauvignon to make dry, crisp, elegant Graves and succulently sweet Sauternes. In Australia it's often mixed with Chardonnay to make wines with a tropical fruity flavour; and where it is allowed to be a star in its own right it has a wonderful depth and sweetness, a bit like very ripe pineapple.

Wine buff's tip

Wines based on Sémillon can age for decades. A 1784 bottle of the famous dessert wine Château d'Yquem fetched £36,000 at London auction house Christie's in 1986.

Aussie Sémillon or Sémillon blends go well with slightly spicy, southeast-Asian food. Sauternes is a classic dessert wine but is sometimes partnered with *foie gras* (the great French delicacy of fattened goose liver) and Roquefort, the famous French blue cheese.

Good value Sémillon comes from: Australia.

Gamay
(one wine that is pronounced as it looks – *Ga-may*)

Gamay is the fruitiest of grapes; the grape that goes to make the light, fresh, raspberryish wines of Beaujolais. Although it can be serious, it's best known as Beaujolais Nouveau – the first wine of the new

harvest, a blissful breath of summery relief during the dark days of
November.

Gamay is wonderful with French charcuterie – a plate of rough
mountain sausage, a slab of pâté and a hunk of fresh, crusty bread. It's
one of the rare red wines that are just as good served lightly chilled.

Good value Gamay comes from: France.

Pinot Noir
(pee-no nwah)

In contrast to Gamay, Pinot Noir is the most sophisticated of grapes
which goes to make some of the most expensive red wines in the
world: the great French red Burgundies. It's not just the gloriously
succulent, almost sweet taste of Pinot Noir that's so appealing; it's the
wonderfully voluptuous, silky, smooth texture.

Unfortunately, because it's a bit of a precious, temperamental kind
of a grape, it's hard to grow and doesn't come cheap – except in
Romania, which manages to produce a Pinot Noir which makes up
in robust fruitiness what it lacks in subtlety. The Californians also
make some stunningly good Pinot – at a price.

Because you're likely to have paid a fair amount for a bottle,
don't kill it with strong-flavoured food. Good Pinot Noir is best with
plainly cooked steak and
roasts, and can be magic
with game.

**Good value Pinot Noir
comes from:** Romania,
California, France.

Wine buff's tip

As well as making red wines, Pinot
Noir is somewhat surprisingly used in a
good deal of Champagne, adding body
and character to the Chardonnay grape.

CHAPTER 7

What's In a Name?

By now you can walk into a wine shop and recognise at least a third of the wine on the shelves. This chapter, which is unavoidably a long one which you may like to take in chunks, is about recognising the next third. To do that, you need to be familiar with a few key names.

Unfortunately, not all wines fall conveniently into single grape varieties. A great many are blends of more than one variety, some very obscure. (The famous French wine Châteauneuf–du–Pape, for instance, can contain up to thirteen varieties.) Some of these wines have been mentioned already in Chapter 2, but in this chapter you'll meet others you're likely to come across.

It's also useful to be able to recognise the names of some of the companies and people who produce the wines, particularly in the New World where the only way you can distinguish between one Chardonnay and another is by who has made it. The chances are that once you've found one wine you like from a producer you'll like other wines they have made.

Flying winemakers

In the past, wine was made by people who had worked in the same area for years; in the case of France, often centuries. Nowadays, winemakers jet all over the world putting their skills to use making wine for different people. You get Australians making wine in France (a case of taking coals to Newcastle if ever there was one), the French making wine in South America and an Englishman making wine in Moldova.

The characteristic of all these wines is that they are very approachable, upfront and fruity. If you discover a winemaker whose wines you like, follow him around the globe.

Five Flying Winemakers

Hugh Ryman (English): all over France, Germany, Hungary,

Moldova, Spain, Chile.

Kym Milne (Australian): Bulgaria, Germany, Hungary, South Africa, Italy.

Jacques Lurton (French): Australia, Argentina, France, Italy, Spain.

Mark Robertson (New Zealand): France (Provence).

Nick Butler (Australian): Hungary, Czech Republic.

Names To Look Out For

France

France is best known for its famous wines, many of which have already been mentioned in Chapter 2. But there is a wealth of less familiar wines that are good value and don't fall into any well known wine regions. They're usually referred to as French country wines.

There are two important areas which produce most of the best known country wines: South West France, the area to the south and southeast of Bordeaux, and the Languedoc down in the far south.

South West France

Being near Bordeaux, the wines from the South West are very similar in style to Bordeaux wines. The whites, of which the best known are Bergerac and Côtes de Duras, are light, crisp and lemony. The reds, which include Bergerac and Buzet, are rich, smooth and fruity; like a claret, but quite often cheaper. There are also some rich full-bodied reds from this area, of which the best known is Cahors. Other names to look out for are Vin de  Pays de Côtes de Gascogne, Vin de Pays du Gers, and Gaillac (all three of them white and red).

Languedoc Roussillon (*Long-ger-doc roo-see-yong*)
The Languedoc is a huge wine-growing area running up to
Provence in the east and down to the Spanish border, where some of
the most exciting new wines in France are being produced. Many of
these are labelled with the grape variety, but you will also see the
descriptions Vin de Pays d'Oc and Coteaux du Languedoc on wines
from this region.

The Languedoc's great strength is its wonderfully powerful gutsy
reds, of which the best known are Corbières, Fitou and Minervois.
St-Chinian and Faugères are also excellent. Other *vin de pays* wines
from this region are Vin de Pays de l'Aude, Vin de Pays de l'Hérault
and Vin de Pays du Gard. Côtes du Roussillon produces
comparatively light, fruity reds.

French Wine Descriptions

There are so many different kinds of French wine descriptions,
it can be very confusing. The ones you are likely to see most
often are *Vin de Pays* and *Appellation Contrôlée* or AC.

■ *Vin de Pays* officially indicates a level of quality higher than a
vin de table, or table wine, but because they are not subject to
the same restrictions as an AC wine, many leading winemakers
use this description of their top quality wines.

■ *Appellation Contrôlée* is the top ranking for French wines,
covering every type of wine from a major Bordeaux area like
Pauillac to a small production area like Faugères. The important
thing to remember is that the authorities lay down rules about
the way the wine is made and the grapes that can be used, to
ensure that the wine has a recognisable character.

You may less frequently see the description VDQS (*Vin
Délimité de Qualité Supérieure*) which is the next official quality
level between Vin de Pays and AC wines.

Bordeaux (*Board-oh*)
Bordeaux is one of the hardest wine regions to get to grips with. A

massive wine-producing area, twice the size of all Australia's vineyards put together, it produces a quarter of France's top quality wine.

Claret, the famous red wine of Bordeaux, accounts for three quarters of all the wine produced in the region – the rest being made up of elegant, dry whites and the most glorious sweet wines in the world (see Chapter 10).

The classic red Bordeaux blend is a mixture of Cabernet Sauvignon, Merlot and another grape called Cabernet Franc, the exact proportions of which depend where in the area it is made. Smooth, rich and velvety in style, it has inspired winemakers all over the world to copy it.

The easiest names to recognise are the main *appellations*, the most important of which is the Médoc. This big area contains four famous villages – Margaux, Pauillac, St-Estèphe and St-Julien. The two other top areas are St-Émilion and Pomerol. Graves produces fine reds as well as some of the best dry white wines in France. Côtes du Bourg and Fronsac are two more moderately priced clarets to look out for, while the huge Entre-Deux-Mers region produces most of Bordeaux' inexpensive reds and whites.

Bordeaux winespeak

Bordeaux wine labels are littered with descriptions such as *Grand*, *Premier* and *Supérieur*, which inconveniently mean slightly different things in different areas. The two worth remembering are *Cru Bourgeois*, which generally indicates a serious wine, and the five great *Crus Classés* (or 'classed growths') which really are the bee's knees. Just for reference, in case you win the pools, the top five *Premier Cru* ('first growth') wines are Châteaux Lafite, Latour, Margaux, Haut-Brion and Mouton-Rothschild.

GRAND VIN DE BORDEAUX

MIS EN BOUTEILLES AU CHÂTEAU

CHATEAU CARIGNAN
PREMIERE COTE DE BORDEAUX
APPELLATION PREMIERE COTE DE BORDEAUX CONTROLEE
1990
12% vol.   G. F. A. Philippe Pieraerts   750ml
Propriétaire à Carignan de Bordeaux (Gironde)

PRODUCE OF FRANCE

Burgundy

Burgundy is made on the other side of France to Bordeaux, but like Bordeaux is highly regarded and can be highly expensive. Both red and white Burgundy are good; the wines most people have heard of are Chablis (white) and Nuits-St-Georges (red). For better value (but we're still not talking cheap), look out for some of the lesser known Burgundies and for the names of well known producers and *négociants* (men who buy basic wine in from small growers and blend it into great wine).

The Côtes
Almost everywhere in Burgundy seems to begin with Côte. The most important wine-producing area is the Côte d'Or, which contains two key areas you may find referred to on bottles: Côtes de Nuits and Côtes de Beaune. (*Côte*, incidentally, is the French word for slope, many vineyards being planted on the side of a hill.)

Basic characteristics of Burgundy
White Burgundy is at its most expensive if Chardonnay is at its peak. This is where the great dry white wines of the world are made, crisp and elegant when young but ageing to a glorious rich, creamy, nutty fullness. Similarly, the great red Burgundies are the best wines made out of the Pinot Noir grape: smooth, silky, sumptuous and lingering. Unfortunately, basic inexpensive Burgundy doesn't hit these heights; you do have to pay over the odds to get the real thing.

Lesser known white Burgundies to look out for are Mercurey, Montagny, Pouilly-Fuissé, Rully and St-Véran. Great white Burgundies (but we're talking megabucks) include Corton-Charlemagne, Meursault and Puligny-Montrachet.

Lesser known red Burgundies to spot are Beaune, Fixin, Givry, Mercurey and Rully (again) and Santenay. Great red Burgundies include Gevrey-Chambertin, Volnay and Vosne-Romanée.

Best known growers and dealers: Bouchard Père et Fils, Drouhin, Jadot, Jaffelin, Latour.

Beaujolais *(Bow-jollay)*
Best known for basic red Beaujolais and Beaujolais Nouveau, it's easy to overlook the fact that there are some serious wines in the region. Known as *Cru Beaujolais* (to indicate that they're higher quality), they still have that lovely fresh raspberryish character, but also a depth of flavour that basic Beaujolais doesn't possess. The most familiar are Brouilly, Chiroubles, Fleurie, Juliénas, Morgon and Moulin-à-Vent.

The best known producer in Beaujolais (sometimes referred to as the 'King of Beaujolais') is Georges Duboeuf.

Wine buff's tip

The word *villages (veelarj)* after Beaujolais (and Côtes du Rhône) means that the wine comes from specific villages in the region and is of a higher quality.

The Rhône (*Rone*)

Although this southern French region is best known for light, easy drinking red Côtes du Rhône, its real strength is in its big, serious, rich fruity reds of which the best known is Châteauneuf-du-Pape. There is also good value to be found among the lesser known Rhône wines (although some like Hermitage and Côte Rôtie are expensive).

Good, lesser known Rhône wines: Cornas, Crozes-Hermitage, Gigondas, Lirac, St-Joseph, Vacqueyras.
Inexpensive country wines from the Rhône and Provence: As well as Côtes du Rhône, look out for Côtes du Ventoux and Côtes du Luberon (which comes from Peter Mayle – *A Year in Provence* – country).

Wine buff's tip

Although the Rhône is primarily red wine country, there are also some white wines made, the most fabulous and rarest of which is Condrieu, which is made from the Viognier grape.

Best known Rhône producers: Paul Jaboulet Ainé, Chapoutier, Guigal.

The Loire

The Loire is famous for its white wines, the best known of which are Sancerre and Pouilly-Fumé (both made from the Sauvignon grape), crisp, dry Muscadet and soft, honeyed Vouvray. Less well known is that it makes some light, fruity, elegant reds.

Wine buff's tip

Muscadet is often described on the bottle as *'sur lie'*, which refers to the way it is made - leaving the wine in contact with its 'lees' or sediment. This gives it a richer, slightly yeasty flavour. Nowadays you can find *sur lie* wines from other areas of France.

Lesser known white wines to look out for are Menetou-Salon, Quincy and inexpensive Sauvignon de Touraine: a not-to-be-despised poor man's Sancerre.
Good Loire reds are Bourgueil, Chinon, Sancerre and Saumur-Champigny. There is also some rosé made, the best known of which is Rosé d'Anjou (more on rosés on page 70).

Alsace

Alsace wines look and often sound like German wines but they have their own distinct character. At the expensive end (the Rieslings and Gewürztraminers) they can be very great wines indeed.

Most Alsace wines are white and labelled with the grape variety they are made from:

Pinot Blanc (*pee-no blong*) - a soft, well-rounded dry white.
Pinot Gris (*pee-no gree*) - a slightly more complex wine, still dry but with refreshing acidity.
Sylvaner (*sill-vama*) - just off dry, slightly aromatic wine.
Muscat (*musk-cat*) - a light, fragrant, dry wine made from the Muscat grape.
Riesling (*ree-sling*) - generally more powerful, intense and less flowery than the German variety.
Gewürztraminer (*ger-vurz-trameana*) - an exotic, rich, spicy dry wine.
Best known Alsace producers: Hugel, Trimbach, Turckheim.

Germany

If names are tricky in Bordeaux they are a nightmare in Germany, which is probably why people never get round to buying the less familiar wines and why they remain so underrated.

Almost all German wine is white, though there is the odd soft fruity red (like Dornfelder). Apart from the familiar Liebfraumilch, and Riesling (the most popular German grape), the most useful names to remember are those that relate to the levels of sweetness in the wine, which are explained in Chapter 10. Look out too for the words *trocken* (dry) and *halb trocken* (half dry) – or in other words, medium sweet.

German wine regions

It can also be helpful to know the main wine-growing areas, several of which begin with *Rhein* (because they border the River Rhine):

Baden is one of the only areas to make dry white wines.

Mosel-Saar-Ruwer makes some of the most beautifully light, elegant (and expensive) Rieslings in Germany. Inexpensive Piesporter also comes from this region.

Rheingau is generally considered the greatest, most prestigious wine-growing area in Germany, making fuller, more intense wines than the Mosel.

Rheinhessen is home to some of the more inexpensive wines like Niersteiner Gutes Domtal.

Rheinpfalz makes a mixture of expensive and inexpensive wines, but is tipped as the up-and-coming German wine region.

The *Nahe* region also produces both cheaper and more expensive wines; and you may come across the word *Bereich*, which refers to a specific area or group of villages.

German winespeak

Germany has a bewildering system of classification for its wines but letters to look out for are QbA (*Qualitätswein bestimmte Anbaugebiete*, in case you want to drop it into your conversation), which stands for quality wine from a designated region, and QmP (*Qualitätswein mit Prädikat*) which indicates a better quality wine than the basic table wine (*Tafelwein*). QmP is much higher quality than QbA.

Italy

Most of us are quite familiar with the names of Italian wines. You'd probably have no trouble in naming half a dozen: Frascati, Soave, Lambrusco, Chianti, Valpolicella and Asti Spumante spring pretty readily to mind. The problem is the rest aren't quite so memorable and don't fit neatly into grape varieties or regions the way other countries' wines do.

The easiest way to remember Italian wines is by the style, and conveniently they fall into three main groups:

Light dry whites: These include

Product of Italy

Soave

Denominazione di Origine Controllata

A Crisp Dry White Wine

BOTTLED BY
FRATELLI PASQUA S.p.A. VERONA - ITALIA

75 d e   11.5% vol

Bianco di Custoza, Frascati, Orvieto and Pinot Grigio. Soave is slightly fuller and rounder. Three lesser known but interesting dry Italian whites worth trying are Gavi, Lugana and Vernaccia di San Gimignano, a crisp dry white from Tuscany, where Chianti comes from.

Light to medium-bodied fruity reds: Barbera, Bardolino, Montepulciano d'Abruzzo, Rosso Conero, Rosso di Montalcino, Valpolicella, and young, inexpensive Chianti. (Rosso means red.)

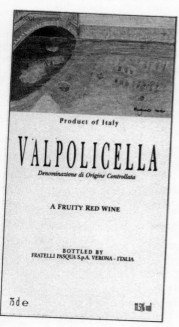

Product of Italy

VALPOLICELLA

Denominazione di Origine Controllata

A FRUITY RED WINE

BOTTLED BY
FRATELLI PASQUA S.p.A. VERONA - ITALIA

75 d e   11.5% vol

Full, powerful reds: More mature, expensive Chianti, Copertino, Barolo, Barbaresco and Brunello di Montalcino (one of Italy's most expensive reds).

Italian winespeak

Italy has an equivalent of the French wine laws called DOC (*Denominazione di Origine Controllata*), but many trendy Italian winemakers prefer not to abide by the rules and use the description *Vino da Tavola* (table wine) to describe their designer wines. Wines described as *Classico* usually come from the best vineyards in the area, while *Superiore* means the wine has more alcohol than the basic version, not necessarily that it's superior.

Two Italian grapes to remember

While some of Italy's best known wines, such as Barbera and Pinot Grigio, are already named after the grape they are made from, there are two Italian grapes which are beginning to appear on labels in their own right: Sangiovese (*san-geeo-vaysi*), the main grape used in Chianti, and Primitivo (*prim-it-teavo*), a grape which makes a gutsy red a bit like the Californian Zinfandel.

Best known Italian producers: Anselmi, Antinori, Masi, Umani Ronchi and Zenato.

Spain

Spain has undergone a revolution in wine-making that makes it hard to associate a name with a style. The famous Spanish red Rioja, for instance, used to be heavy and oaky. Nowadays it can be vibrantly fresh and fruity (though the oaky versions still exist).

As with Italian wines, it's easiest to look at Spanish wines in three main groups:

Wine buff's tip

The best known Spanish grape is Tempranillo which crops up in Rioja and other strong Spanish reds. Confusingly, it is sometimes known by other names such as Cencibel.

Inexpensive fruity red and white wines: These are up-to-the-minute wines made in an easy drinking style. Look for wines from La Mancha, Navarra, Valdepeñas and Valencia.

More traditional, but still inexpensive Spanish wines:
These are wines which have a typical Spanish character. Rueda, a dry full-bodied wine is the best known white. More traditional oaky reds include Leon, Jumilla and Toro.

More expensive Spanish wines, made in a modern style:
There has also been a revolution at the top end of Spanish wines, with winemakers like Raimat and Miguel Torres turning out sophisticated wines, often from a named grape variety like Cabernet or Merlot.

Rioja (*ree-och-ar*)

Rioja is generally thought of as red, but there is also white Rioja. Like the reds, it used to be considered old fashioned but there is a demand once again for elegant, crisp, fruity whites.

You can tell how oaky a Rioja is going to be by the label. If the wine is described as a *Crianza*, it means it will be at least three years old and have spent a minimum of twelve months in oak (six months in the case of a white). A *Reserva* will be at least five years old and have spent twelve months in oak. A *Gran Reserva* will be at least six years old and have spent two years in oak.

Best known Rioja producers: Campillo, Campo Viejo, Contino, CVNE, Marques de Caceres, Marques de Murrieta, Marques de Riscal.

Portugal

Apart from port, Portugal has two well known wines: Mateus Rosé and Vinho Verde, a light, crisp dry white. Like Spain, Portuguese wine-making has come on in leaps and bounds, with fresher, fruitier wines replacing traditional oaky reds. Inexpensive wines to look out for include Bairrada, Dão, Douro and Leziria.

Portugal also produces some fine, mature, richly flavoured reds which are excellent value for money compared to similar wines from other parts of the world. A well known example is Tinto da Anfora. Wines labelled *Garrafeira* are high quality wines which have been aged in oak for at least two years (six months for whites).

Wine buff's tip

Two Portuguese grapes to look out for on bottles are Fernao Pires (a white grape making dry full-flavoured whites) and Periquita, which is used to make full, fruity reds. The Alentejo is widely tipped as the up-and-coming wine region.

Best known Portuguese producers: Fonseca, Sogrape, J.P.Vinhos.

Eastern Europe

A source of excellent inexpensive drinking, the most useful thing to remember about Eastern Europe is its grapes (see Chapter 2). Look out too for wines made by flying winemakers like Hugh Ryman, Kym Milne and Nick Butler.

England

English wines are generally made from tricky-to-remember German grapes. The best known producer is Denbies, but look out too for wines produced by the Harvest Wine Group under the direction of Australian winemaker John Worontschak. Names to spot are Thames Valley, Penn, Pilton Manor and Sharpham.

The New World

Australia

Thinking of Australian wines as all the same is like lumping the wines of France, Italy, Spain and Portugal together. There are regional differences but perhaps even more important is the talent of individual winemakers, who can often make a silk purse out of a sow's ear in coping with the difficult wine-growing conditions. (Australia is hot

1992

Nottage Hill

SOUTH EASTERN
AUSTRALIA
CABERNET SAUVIGNON

for a wine-producing country, hence all that big fruit flavour.)

Best known wine regions

Most Australian wine comes from South Australia (around Adelaide) which includes the famous Barossa Valley. Other important areas you may see on a bottle are Coonawarra (particularly for reds) and Padthaway (for whites). Most of the rest comes from next-door New South Wales (the area around Sydney) whose most famous region is the Hunter Valley.

Best known Australian producers and brands

Penfolds is the biggest name among the producers, a vast group which includes other well known companies like Lindemans, Seaview and Seppelts, and brand names like Koonunga Hill. Jacob's Creek is Australia's best-selling wine, while other names you may come across are Hardy's (who produce Nottage Hill and Moondah Brook wines), Brown Brothers, Rosemount, and – at the slightly pricier end – Wolf Blass and Krondorf.

What does Bin on a wine label mean?

You'll often see the word Bin and then a number – like Bin 28 or Bin 65 – on Australian wines. Originally, it was simply a device for keeping the different batches of grapes apart

Wine buff's tip

Two top Australian wines are Grange (also called Grange Hermitage), a smooth, sophisticated red made from seventy-year-old Shiraz vines, and Pyrus - both made in the style of top Bordeaux.

in the winery, now it's used to identify the various batches of wine.

Best known Australian winemakers

In Australia, winemakers are celebrities, larger-than-life characters whose sheer personality sells their wines. Look out for wines made by Brian Croser (Petaluma), Len Evans, winemaker and writer James Halliday (Coldstream Hills), Bob McLean (St Hallett) and moustachioed Geoff Merrill, the self-styled 'Wizard of Oz'.

New Zealand

Less famous than its glamorous neighbour, New Zealand nevertheless produces wines of just as high a quality. Although best known for its extraordinarily intense Sauvignon Blancs, look out too for New Zealand Chardonnay, Cabernet and Merlot, and first-class sparklers (see Chapter 9).

COOKS
ENDEAVOUR COLLECTION
CABERNET SAUVIGNON PINOT NOIR
GISBORNE
1992   75cl℮
WINE OF
NEW ZEALAND
11.5%vol
HMS ENDEAVOUR
PRODUCED BY COOKS WINE COMPANY AUCKLAND

Best known wine regions
Marlborough (South Island) - the biggest wine region, best known for its Sauvignons.
Gisborne (North Island) - the most productive region, producing good-value inexpensive wines.
Hawkes Bay (North Island) - produces some of the best quality New Zealand wines.

Best known New Zealand producers: Cooks, Montana, Nobilo, Villa Maria.

Wine buff's tip

The state-of-the-art New Zealand Sauvignon Blanc is Cloudy Bay, a rival to the great Loire Sauvignons like Sancerre and Pouilly-Fumé. Other top Sauvignons are Delegats, Jackson Estate, Stoneleigh and Vidal.

California

California has always looked to France for inspiration, and with typical energy set out to beat the French at their own game. As with other New World countries, the easiest approach to Californian wines is to concentrate on the grapes, though there are a few big names worth remembering.

Best known wine regions

The most famous region in California is the Napa Valley, just north of San Francisco, which produces many of California's quality red wines. Sonoma County, next door, is also an important wine-producing area.

Best known Californian producers

Streets ahead of any other producer in terms of size is Gallo, which produces a quarter of all the wine in the United States. High quality producers include Beringer, Fetzer and Robert Mondavi.

California's own grape

As well as the major grape varieties, California grows Zinfandel, which makes a rich, spicy, full-flavoured red wine. Well known producers include Fetzer, Inglenook and (more expensively) Ridge.

Wine buff's tip

One of California's most expensive wines is Opus One, the classic French
claret blend of Cabernet Sauvignon and Merlot produced by a partnership
between Robert Mondavi and Baron Philippe de Rothschild, one of Bordeaux'
most famous wine producers.

Chile

1993
MAULE VALLEY

MERLOT

GROWN, PRODUCED AND BOTTLED BY
VIÑA ERRAZURIZ PANQUEHUE · PRODUCT OF CHILE

13.0% vol.   75 cl.e

Again, most of Chile's wines
are labelled with the grape
variety. The two best known
wine regions are Curicó and
Maipo, but watch out for
white wines from the
Casablanca region, tipped as
the most promising area.

**Best known Chilean
producers and brands:**
Caliterra, Concha y Toro,
Errazuriz and Montes (where
flying winemaker Hugh
Ryman has been lending a
hand).

South Africa

Most wine in South Africa is made around Cape Town, which is
why you often see the word Cape as part of the name. Wine-
growing areas that you may see on the label are Robertson
(particularly on white wines), Stellenbosch and Paarl.

Best known South African producers

Most South African wine used to come from the KWV, a massive group of producers. Nowadays the more expensive wines tend to come from individual estates like Fairview, Kanonkop and Van Loveren.

Also look out for wines made by three of the great characters of South African wine-making: Jan Coetzee, Neil Ellis and Danie de Wet – all ex-rugby players!

Wine buff's tip

The first wine of the year is not Beaujolais Nouveau but a wine from the New World, where they have their harvest six months earlier. Beating most of them to the tape is South Africa's Goiya Kgeisje (pronounced *Hoya heysee*, meaning 'first wine'), a crisp, citrussy white.

At-a-glance Guide to the World's Best Known Grapes and Wines

White Wine Grapes	Old World	New World
Chardonnay	France: White Burgundy (eg Chablis); Pays d'Oc Hungary	Australia California Chile New Zealand South Africa
Chenin Blanc	France: The Loire (eg Vouvray)	South Africa
Colombard	France: Vin de Pays des Côtes de Gascogne	South Africa
Gewürztraminer	France: Alsace	
Pinot Blanc	France: Alsace Italy: Pinot Bianco Hungary	
Pinot Gris	France: Alsace Italy: Pinot Grigio	
Riesling	Germany France: Alsace	Australia
Sauvignon	France: The Loire (eg Sancerre, Pouilly-Fumé); Bordeaux (eg Graves) where it is blended with Sémillon and white Bordeaux-type blends (eg Bergerac, Côtes de Duras)	California (where it is sometimes called Fumé Blanc); Chile New Zealand
Sémillon	France: In sweet wines (eg Sauternes, Barsac) and as part of dry white Bordeaux blends (see above)	Australia: On its own or blended with Chardonnay

Red Wine Grapes	Old World	New World
Cabernet Sauvignon	France: Bordeaux (blended with Cabernet Franc and Merlot), and in Bordeaux-type blends (eg Bergerac, Buzet) Bulgaria Hungary Spain	Australia California Chile New Zealand South Africa
Cabernet Franc	France: In Bordeaux blends (see above); Loire reds (eg Bourgeuil, Chinon)	
Gamay	France: Beaujolais	
Merlot	France: In Bordeaux blends (see above); Pays d'Oc Italy Hungary	Chile New Zealand
Pinotage		South Africa
Pinot Noir	France: Red Burgundy Romania	California
Sangiovese	Italy: eg Chianti	California
Shiraz (in France, known as Syrah)	France: The Rhône (eg Hermitage, Châteauneuf-du-Pape); the Languedoc	Australia: on its own or blended with Cabernet Sauvignon; South Africa
Tempranillo	Spain: eg Rioja	
Zinfandel		California

Countries listed are the main ones in which you'll find each grape.

CHAPTER 8

Finding your Wine Style

Sooner or later we all find a wine we really like. But rather than drink the same bottle every time, it's fun to experiment with different wines without letting yourself in for a shock. To do that, it helps to find which other bottles have a similar taste to your favourite – that is, to find your preferred wine style.

Four factors that affect a wine style

Oak

Whether a wine is light or full-bodied depends a great deal on whether it has been oaked. Traditionally, this meant the wine being kept in oak barrels; nowadays winemakers can simply dangle a few oak chips in a vat of wine to get an oaky effect.

The barrels in which wine was aged used to be kept for years and years so the wines became very oaky and tannic. Today many wines are aged in new oak or barrels that are only a few years old, which gives a rich toasty flavour to white wines like Chardonnay and doesn't overwhelm the fruit in reds like Cabernet Sauvignon and Shiraz.

A winemaker can determine how oaky – or heavy – his wine will be by the amount of time it spends in the barrel. A Chardonnay may only spend two to three months in oak. A Chianti or Rioja can spend two to three years.

Using oak is expensive and pushes up the price of a bottle. Since the winemaker is offering a higher quality wine, he will generally boast about it on the label.

Age

Age has a major role to play in the texture of a wine. Wines from the most recent vintage will be (or ought to be) fresh and fruity, though whites that have just been bottled can occasionally taste a bit 'green' or sour, and reds a bit rough and stalky.

With age the rough edges soften out, and wines that are a couple of years old are generally rounder, smoother and fuller, though there are some white wines and young reds that don't benefit from keeping even that long (see Chapter 4).

The odd thing is that wines that are kept for a really long time, like claret, Burgundy and Rioja, become less heavy, fade in colour and gain a curious sweetness and intensity. This is either a taste you like or you don't like; if you're not mad about oaked wines, you probably won't take to them.

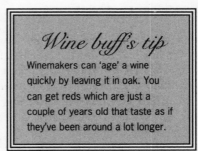

Wine buff's tip

Winemakers can 'age' a wine quickly by leaving it in oak. You can get reds which are just a couple of years old that taste as if they've been around a lot longer.

Sweetness

Sweetness is the issue that divides most wine drinkers. Again, it's very much a matter of personal taste. Most white wines nowadays (except German) are made dry, but they're also made fruity which pleases the palate of those who have a sweet tooth. Dessert wines are made deliberately sweet (more on those in Chapter 10).

Alcohol level

Very simple, this: light wines are low in alcohol. Heavy, full-flavoured wines are high in alcohol. Light wines – white or red – are generally 11, 11.5 or 12 per cent; heavy wines between 12 and 13.5 per cent (see Chapter 22).

Experimenting with wine styles

By and large, most wine falls into one of the following categories, although you may always find a wine of a particular type made in a slightly different style. The pound signs give you an idea of the price bracket they fall into: **£** indicates wines round about the £3 mark; **££** means you should be able to find them for under £5; and **£££** represents more expensive wines over £5.

White wines

Light, dry whites – fresh, crisp whites sometimes with a touch of lemon, almonds or a slight earthy tang. Muscadet is a classic example.
£ Inexpensive Italian whites such as Pinot Grigio and Bianco di Custoza.
££ Muscadet and other *sur lie* wines, Italian Soave, Spanish Rueda, Portuguese Vinho Verde and Terret – a dry earthy white from the South of France.

Light, flowery whites – these are the wines to try if you like Liebfraumilch.
£ Inexpensive German whites such as Liebfraumilch, Hock and Piesporter. Bulgarian and Hungarian country whites. Slightly fuller, fruitier whites such as Vin de Pays des Côtes de Gascogne and South African Colombard.
££ or £££ Try an English white wine or a light German Riesling.

Sharp, lemony whites – these are wines to try if you like unsweetened lemon juice, grapefruit and gooseberries. Sauvignon Blanc is the grape to look for.
£ Inexpensive Sauvignons from Hungary and South Africa, French Bergerac and Côtes de Duras, Portuguese Bairrada.
££ Sauvignons from New Zealand, southern France (the Pays d'Oc), Chile.
£££ Classic Sauvignons from the Loire, eg Sancerre and Pouilly-Fumé.

Smooth, full, well-rounded whites – although dry, these wines also have body and fullness. The classic example is Chablis, but you'll also like most unoaked Chardonnays.
£ Hungarian Chardonnay, South African Chenin Blanc.
££ Chardonnay from Italy, South Africa and the Pays d'Oc in southern France. Alsace Pinot Blanc.
£££ Chablis and other white Burgundies, white Graves (from the Bordeaux region).

Rich, fruity, oaky whites – big powerful whites, rich in tropical fruit, oak and alcohol. Look for Australian and other New

World Chardonnays.

££ or £££ Chardonnay from Australia, California, Chile and New Zealand. Also Sémillon and Sémillon/Chardonnay blends.

Complex, spicy whites – wines with an aromatic, spicy rather than a fruity character. Often very successful with spicy food.

£ Irsai Oliver and dry Muscat from Hungary.

££ or £££ Gewürztraminer and Riesling from Alsace; some of the pricier German Rieslings which have a strange, aromatic, almost oily smell and texture, which tastes a good deal nicer than it sounds.

> ## *Wine buff's tip*
> You can tell the style of white wines by the colour. Lighter wines tend to have a pale straw colour, citrussy wines like Sauvignons are often greeny-yellow, while fuller-flavoured oaky Chardonnays are a rich gold. Generally, the lighter the colour, the lighter the wine.

Off-dry/semi-sweet whites – soft, honeyed, but not as sweet as a dessert wine.

£ Inexpensive *halb trocken* German whites, Morio Muskat.

££ Australian Rhine Riesling, wines labelled 'medium dry'.

£££ Semi-sweet (*demi-sec*) wines from the Loire region of France, such as Vouvray.

Red wines

Light reds – light, fresh, cherryish reds, like Beaujolais, which can even be served chilled.

£ Young reds from Bulgaria and Hungary, inexpensive Valpolicella.

££ Beaujolais and other Gamay wines.

£££ Red wines from the Loire region of France.

Medium–bodied, fruity reds – not weighty wines but with plenty of ripe fruit, such as wines made from the Merlot grape.

£ Inexpensive Spanish reds (Navarra, Valdepeñas). Italian and Hungarian Merlot, French country wines.

££ Côtes du Rhône, basic Burgundy, South African Pinotage.
£££ More expensive Beaujolais and Burgundy from recent vintages.

Rich, smooth reds – smoothness is the keynote of this type of wine which has an intense fruit flavour, not overwhelmed by oak. If you like the blackcurranty flavour of Cabernet Sauvignon, you'll like this style of wine.
£ Bulgarian or Hungarian Cabernet Sauvignon (but not reserve wines which will have a strong oaky character).
££ Claret; Australian, Chilean, New Zealand or South African Cabernet Sauvignon or Cabernet blends. Good quality Chianti.
£££ More expensive clarets and New World Cabernet Sauvignon, Californian Pinot Noir, and expensive French Burgundy.

Big, gutsy reds – the characteristic of this kind of wine is its sheer power. Likely to have been oaked, it may also have a touch of spiciness. Good examples are Shiraz and Rhône wines made from the Syrah grape.
£ More traditionally made Spanish and Portuguese reds like Toro and Dão.
££ Southern French wines from the Languedoc such as Fitou and St-Chinian. Australian or South African Shiraz. Wines made from the Tempranillo grape in Spain. Californian Zinfandel.
£££ Classic Rhône wines like Châteauneuf-du-Pape and Crozes-Hermitage. Italian Barolo.

Aged or very oaky reds – the wine develops a kind of sweetness, either from age or being left in wood for a long time. You rarely find this style in New World wines.
£ Bulgarian reserve wines.
££ Wines from the southern 'heel' of Italy like Copertino, Squinzano, and Salice Salentino.
£££ Old Burgundy, claret and Rioja.

Rosés
Rosé has never really been taken seriously, and on the whole rightly. For years it was bland and sugary-sweet. Suddenly, however, winemakers seem to have taken a shine to it, and it's back in fashion again. The new rosés are quite a different kettle of fish to the old,

ranging from light, elegant wines with a lovely whiff of strawberries, to quite robust beefy rosés which will stand up well to food.

How do I tell which kind of rosé is which?

There's a lot of experimenting going on at the moment, so it's difficult to give hard and fast guidance. It's best to check the back label, where there is one, which should tell you the style in which the wine was made. Failing that, look for:

■ *the colour* – by and large, rosés that are a pale peach or sweet candyfloss pink will be sweeter than those which are a fuller, richer colour;
■ *the name of the grape* – rosés made from red wine grapes like Syrah and Cabernet Sauvignon are likely to be drier and more full-bodied;
■ *the alcohol content* – the higher the alcohol level, the stronger the wine.

Wine buff's tip

Rosés should be treated like white wine. Drink them cold.

Rosés also go by different names, depending on the country you're in. In Spain and Portugal it's *rosado*, while Italian rosés are called *rosato*. The Californians (and now some other winemakers) call theirs *blush*.

PART III

Pushing The Boat Out

CHAPTER 9

Fantastic Fizz

While most of the time you will be drinking white, red and
occasionally rosé wines, there will be times when you feel like
pushing the boat out a bit – buying a bottle of Champagne, a half
bottle of something deliciously sweet and sticky to drink with an
extra special dessert, or a bottle of port or sherry.

Champagne

If there's one wine that everyone's heard of, it's Champagne. Yet we
don't really think of it as a wine; more like a brand that always tastes
the same. In fact there is more than one style of Champagne, which
tends to depend on the grapes that are used for the blend and the
amount of time the wine is aged.

Surprisingly, most Champagne is made from a white and a red
grape – our old friends Chardonnay and Pinot Noir. A third grape –
another red, Pinot Meunier – can also be added to the blend.
Champagne that is made from Chardonnay alone is called a *Blanc de
Blancs* (literally, a white wine made from white grapes). One that is
made from red grapes alone (though this is less common) is called a
Blanc de Noirs.

The three main Champagne styles

■ Light, citrussy, sometimes appley. Usually a Blanc de Blancs.

■ Dry, rich and toasty. How rich and toasty depends on how long it
has been aged. Good Champagne will often have three years or more
in the bottle.

■ Rosé – dry but can have a touch of strawberry fruit. The pink colour is sometimes added from red grapes, sometimes from a little red wine.

The degrees of sweetness in Champagne are confusing. The driest Champagnes, which make up the majority, are called *brut* (pronounced 'brute'). Champagne described as *sec* (which means dry) is slightly less dry, and *demi-sec* (which means half dry) is in fact sweet.

Is vintage Champagne better than non-vintage?

Not necessarily. Non-vintage doesn't mean a Champagne isn't much good, simply that it's made in a different way. Non-vintage Champagnes are made by blending wines from different vintages and may contain quite a high proportion of old Champagne. The point is to make the blend taste the same each time so customers aren't disappointed.

Vintage Champagnes are made from grapes from a particularly good harvest and producers don't make a vintage every year. They generally are high quality (and therefore more expensive) Champagnes, but that doesn't always mean they're better value.

Best known Champagnes

££ Charles Heidsieck, Lanson, Laurent Perrier, Perrier Jouet, Mercier, Moët, Mumm.
£££ Bollinger, Pol Roger, Veuve Clicquot.
££££ Krug, Roederer.

How much should I pay for a bottle?

Champagne ranges wildly in price from cut-price offers as low as £7.99 or £8.99 up to the dizzy heights of vintage Krug around £60

Wine buff's tip

Britain has always been a great nation of Champagne lovers. During the boom years of the eighties, we sunk about 20 million bottles a year. Now we manage a slightly more modest 15 million - apparently that means a cork pops every two seconds!

or £70. Although the cheaper Champagnes can be excellent value, personally, if I'm going to drink Champagne, I go for the serious stuff at £15 and over, and choose one of the really excellent sparklers from the New World (see below) if I want to be more economical.

How to serve Champagne

Champagne is not best served by jiggling it up and down, racing-driver style, and allowing the cork to go into orbit. For a start, you lose half your Champagne. You should be able to release the cork without making any other noise than a soft *phut*. Follow these three easy steps:

■ Chill the bottle thoroughly first. This makes it safer to open as well as tasting better.

■ Point the bottle at a 45° angle away from your body – and away from anyone else. Take off the foil, and untwist the wire that is holding the cork in place and remove it.

■ Get a good grip on the cork with your left hand (assuming you are right-handed), cupping your palm over the top of the cork, and twist the bottle gently with your right hand until you can feel the cork begin to ease out. Keep a firm grip on it while it pops out (the pressure inside the bottle will do the work for you). This is actually a good deal easier than it sounds, once you get the hang of it.

When you come to pour the Champagne, don't just tip it straight into the glass otherwise the mousse (the bubbles) will froth up and overflow the sides. Hold the glass at a slight angle towards the bottle and pour the Champagne slowly into it.

Champagne is best served out of a tall glass or flute, which traps the bubbles and doesn't allow them to escape as the more old-fashioned saucer-style glass used to.

How to store Champagne

In the unlikely event that you have any Champagne left over, you can either buy a purpose-made Champagne stopper (if you're lucky enough to drink the stuff regularly) or leave an upturned spoon in the neck of the bottle (weird but it works). Either way, refrigerate the leftovers.

Sparklers

Having copied every other kind of French wine, it wasn't likely that the New World were going to leave Champagne alone. And nor have they. The last few years has seen a flood of really excellent copycat wines, particularly from New Zealand, California and, more recently, South Africa.

No one but the Champagne producers can actually put the word Champagne on the bottle, but some of these wines would be hard to tell from the real thing in a blind tasting unless you were a genuine wine buff. Certainly there's no shame these days in offering a sparkler that isn't Champagne.

Good Champagne taste-alikes include Deutz, Lindauer, Mumm Cuvée Napa - some of which are actually made by Champagne producers who have set up shop in the New World. Green Point, for instance, is made by Domaine Chandon, makers of Moët et Chandon.

The French also make sparkling wines that are not Champagne, the best known of which is Veuve du Vernay. Rather more interesting are the Crémant (another term for sparkling) wines, such as Crémant d'Alsace, Crémant de Bourgogne and the little known Crémant de Limoux - a delicious, soft, appley fizz which is supposed to have been the first-ever sparkling wine.

Other dry sparklers

Although these wines are nothing like Champagne - and don't

pretend to be – they're still highly drinkable. Once again, the Aussies lead the field. Look out for well known names like Seaview, Seppelt and Yalumba Angas Brut, and for even cheaper party sparklers which they somehow manage to produce for under a fiver.

The other big producer of sparkling wine is Spain, which has Cava, a very dry, crisp kind of fizz. This used to be fairly cheap and cheerful, but there are now some quite complex versions appearing on the market. Well known names to look for are Cordoniu and Freixenet (pronounced *Fre-zhe-nay*), which comes in a distinctive black bottle.

There are also one or two red sparklers around such as sparkling Shiraz, and even red Lambrusco (the kind the Italians drink), which are fun to take on a summer picnic.

Soft, sweet sparklers

The Italians are head-and-shoulders leaders in this field with their famous sweet sparkling wine Asti Spumante. Although wine buffs tend to look down their noses at Asti, it is a marvellous drink, particularly in summer and especially with summer fruit. You should drink it if you like it.

Wine buff's tip

Moscato is the Italian name for the Muscat grape, which is widely used to make sweeter wines (see next chapter). The French also make an excellent sparkler based on Muscat called Clairette de Die.

Less well known are Moscato Spumante (pretty much the same thing but less heavily advertised and therefore less expensive) and – the great bargains of sparkling wine drinking – Moscato D'Asti and Moscato Frizzante, or Moscato Fizz, which are even cheaper. Another delicious, inexpensive Italian sparkler is Prosecco.

CHAPTER 10

Sweet and Sticky

Sweet wines have taken a bit of a knocking in recent years with everyone deciding it's much more sophisticated and stylish to be seen drinking a Chardonnay or Sauvignon Blanc. In the last year or so, however, there have been signs of a comeback, as interest in less usual wines increases.

Sweet wines in fact come in an extraordinary range of styles and flavours, from light and grapey to syrupy lemon-and-honey, to rich, nutty and apricotty, to the wonderfully sticky raisin- and toffee-flavoured marvels which have emerged from Australia (again). Because many of them are so rich and concentrated you need to drink very little, so its best to buy them in half bottles (which are widely available).

> ## *Wine buff's tip*
>
> You may see the term botrytis or botrytised on a bottle of sweet wine. This refers to a natural process of rotting (referred to as noble rot) in which the grapes are deliberately allowed to shrivel on the vine, which concentrates their intensity and sweetness. The term Late Harvest also indicates a sweet wine.

The Muscat grape

Many of these wines are made from the Muscat grape; the only grape of all the ones we've talked about so far that tastes genuinely grapey. It has different names in different countries - Muscat in France and the New World, Moscato in Italy, Moscatel in Spain and Portugal - and makes wine from the lightest fizz to the richest, stickiest Liqueur Muscat.

Probably the best known Muscat is the French Muscat de

Beaumes-de-Venise, an intensely grapey wine which is made down in the Rhône, in the south of France. Similar and cheaper versions are Muscat de Rivesaltes and Muscat de St-Jean-de-Minervois.

Sauternes

The greatest – and most expensive – sweet white wine in the world is Sauternes, which comes from France's great claret region, Bordeaux. Made mainly from the Sémillon grape, with a touch of Sauvignon, the wines are marvellously rich and syrupy, lemon and honeyish, when they're young; rich, nutty and apricotty when they're older. The wine can be aged for a very long time: there are drinkable Château D'Yquems dating back more than a hundred years. A slightly cheaper version of Sauternes is Barsac, which is in the same area.

The three main sweet wine styles

If you want to experiment with sweet wines it's worth sampling at least one from each of these three main wine styles. Remember, all sweet wines (with the exception of Australian Liqueur Muscats, which are delicious at room temperature) should be served well chilled.

Light, fresh and grapey – Inexpensive wines, generally made from the Muscat grape and generally low in alcohol. The classic example is Moscatel de Valencia and the Moscato sparklers mentioned in the last chapter.

Rich, sweet wines – Full, rich dessert wines of which Sauternes is the classic example. Other wines to try are the French Muscats like Muscat de Beaumes-de-Venise, and late harvest Rieslings from Germany, Australia or South Africa.

Intensely concentrated sweet wines – What the Australians call 'stickies', wickedly rich wines with flavours of raisins, toffee, and treacle. As they're high in alcohol, they should be treated as a substitute for sherry or port. Look for the description Liqueur Muscat on the bottle. Well known producers are Baileys, Stanton and Killeen, and Yalumba.

Germany has some extraordinary and often very expensive sweet wines, all with unpronounceable names:

Spätlese (late picked) wines can be sweet but confusingly also dry.

Auslese wines are made from grapes that are specially selected for ripeness; there are some quite inexpensive versions around.

Beerenauslese and **Trockenbeerenauslese** are even sweeter and more intense, made from hand-picked, individually selected grapes. Rare and expensive.

Eiswein, the sweetest and most concentrated of all, is made from grapes that are left to freeze on the vine. Very rare and very expensive.

There are also some excellent, light, elegant, honeyed wines produced in the Loire region of France which don't quite compare with the other types of sweet wine. Names to look out for are Bonnezeaux, Coteaux du Layon and Vouvray (which can also be dry).

CHAPTER 11

Sherry and Port

Sherry and port are so-called 'fortified' wines – wines that have been strengthened with brandy (as some of the earliest wines to be produced, several centuries ago, that was the only way to transport them). The high alcohol content, usually 17 or 18 per cent, also means they keep a long time. They are, in any case, at least three years old by the time they reach the shelf.

Sherry

Sherry, with its stuffy maiden aunt image, surely has to be the world's most underrated wine. We still tend to think of it as sweet and sticky stuff, locked away in the cupboard from one year to the next and only brought out at Christmas as a not-too-daring tipple for elderly relatives. In fact, real sherry as the Spanish drink it is a brilliantly stylish and sophisticated drink that goes with an extraordinarily wide range of food. And because it's not hugely fashionable, it's fantastic value for money.

Spanish-style sherries are much drier than the cream sherries that have traditionally been made for the British market. The three main types are:

Fino – a really bone-dry, tangy sherry that tends, like olives, to be an acquired taste. (It is worth acquiring.) Manzanilla, a type of fino, is if anything even drier, with a pronounced salty tang. Well known finos are La Ina and Tio Pepe.

Amontillado – Spanish-style amontillado is a rich, dry, nutty sherry which may have several years ageing, as opposed to the English style which is much sweeter and has a more caramelly kind of taste.

Oloroso – a deep, raisiny, sweet but not sickly sherry, almost like liquid Christmas cake. Matusalem, an expensive sherry that's worth splashing out on for Christmas, is a classic example.

Well known English-style sherry producers: Croft, Harveys.
Well known Spanish-style sherry producers: Domecq, Garvey, González Byass.

Two golden rules about serving sherry

Serve it cold and drink it quick!

Fino sherries in particular should be treated just like a white wine – chilled in the fridge before opening and consumed within two to three days. Even amontillado sherries will taste better for being lightly chilled, and should be finished within a few weeks. Only rich oloroso sherries taste better warm and have the staying power to remain in good condition for several months.

The best – and least expensive – way to buy sherry is in half bottles, so you're less likely to leave it hanging around.

Sherry glasses

The ideal shape for a sherry glass is not the hour-glass schooner you tend to get in pubs but a small tulip-shaped glass (which you could also use for port). As with other wines, don't fill the glass more than half full.

Wine buff's tip

Real sherry comes from the area immediately round the town of Jerez in the south of Spain (from which sherry got its name). That excludes Montilla, an inexpensive wine made in similar style but produced several miles inland.

British sherry (which is not really sherry at all) will have to stop calling itself that after January 1996 due to pressure from the Spaniards, who get understandably miffed at having their wines compared to a product that simply doesn't compare to the real thing.

Port

Like sherry, port tends to be another once-a-year drink: the traditional finale to the Christmas meal. In fact, that's when you're least likely to appreciate it. It's much better to save it for a special snack with a mince pie or a couple of crackers and a piece of Stilton; or better still, stash it away for a warming winter nightcap to last you through the dark days of January.

And again like sherry, port (which comes from the Douro region in northern Portugal, round Oporto) comes in different styles. The two main types are ruby and tawny:

Ruby port is generally sold quite young (well young in port terms) at about three years, and is

Wine buff's tip

Although port will keep well, it doesn't last forever. If you open a bottle for Christmas, it's best consumed by the spring rather than kept for the following Christmas.

rich and fruity. A bit like a rather nice cough mixture. Longer-matured ruby ports are called vintage character or late bottled vintage (not to be confused with vintage port) and gain extra richness from not being released for 4-6 years.

Tawny port – so called because of its lovely deep amber colour – has a nuttier, more sherry-like flavour. Cheaper tawnies get their colour from a mixture of red and white grapes, while older, more expensive tawnies develop theirs in the barrel over ten, twenty, thirty and even forty years.

You can also buy **white port** which the Portuguese drink as a summer aperitif, topped up with tonic, ice and a slice of lemon.

Vintage port

Vintage port, like vintage Champagne, comes from the grapes of an exceptional year. The port shippers (as the producers are called) only declare (announce) a vintage two or three times a decade. Vintage port needs to be kept for at least ten years, and is frequently kept for longer. Like most old wines, it is an acquired taste. You may well prefer the nutty, creamy flavour of a ten-year-old tawny or the slightly lighter style of a single Quinta (estate) wine.

Do you need to decant port?

Nowadays most ports are produced ready to drink, but older or vintage ports may have some sediment in the bottle. Tackle them the same way you would an old wine (see Chapter 5). One producer (Taylor's) has had the bright idea of producing a nifty little gift pack with a special port filter, to take some of the hassle out of the whole procedure.

Well known port producers

Cockburn's, Croft, Sandeman and Taylor's are the best known producers of modestly priced port. Once you pay a bit more you're spoilt for choice: Dow, Fonseca, Graham, Offley, Smith Woodhouse, Warre, are all well established names.

Other fortified wines: The three Ms

Madeira

There are all sorts of historical and theatrical references to Madeira, which have resulted in it not being taken terribly seriously. In fact, it's every bit as distinguished a wine as its much more famous counter-parts, sherry and port, and can be drunk much the same way.

Basic Madeira, which comes from the island of the same name, is a sweetish, dark, rich wine not dissimilar to a dry oloroso sherry. But there are also four distinct styles of Madeira: Sercial is the driest; Verdelho, medium dry and nutty; Bual, a rich dark Madeira; and Malmsey, which is sweet, treacly and intense.

Due to the very curious way in which it is produced, during which the wine is subject to intense heat for up to six months, Madeira will keep almost indefinitely. You can still find 100- and 150-year-old wines on the market which taste perfectly fresh.

Malaga

Another sweet, rich, treacly fortified wine, made almost next door to sherry in southern Spain. Now something of a rarity.

Marsala

A traditionally dry, nowadays often sweet fortified wine, best known as an ingredient of the famous Italian dessert zabaglione. If you develop a taste for the stuff and want to drink it on its own, look out for the top quality, dry Vergine.

PART IV

Matching Food And Wine

———

CHAPTER 12

Breaking the Rules

Now that you're well on your way to being a wine expert, it's time to tackle the thorny subject of wine with food. It's all very well to pick a bottle to enjoy on its own, but finding the right bottle to go with the food you're eating can be trickier.

The whole exercise is not helped by a lot of so-called 'rules' about which wine to drink with which food. The most famous of these is the 'white wine with fish and red wine with meat' rule. What you have to remember is that this rule was laid down when all British food was pretty plain and wine was almost all French. If you had a bottle of claret, which could be pretty tough and tannic, you had to have a meaty steak or a good old English Sunday roast to set it off. If you had a lightly grilled fillet of plaice and a few boiled potatoes, a crisp, dry Chablis was just the ticket.

Nowadays both wine and food have changed. Instead of grilled steak you're just as likely to be eating a Japanese-style beef teriyaki, while your fish may be marinated and baked in the oven with ginger and garlic. And almost all wines today are made appealingly fresh and fruity, which makes them more flexible partners for different kinds of food.

That's not to say the old rule is completely useless. It's still true that many white wines are too light for meat dishes, while a strong red wine would be totally inappropriate for a stylish, light fish dish. But it's not the most helpful way to approach the subject.

Food changes wine: wine changes food

It sounds ridiculously obvious to say it, but it helps to bear in mind that food generally changes the taste of a wine and wine the taste of a food. Just try this little test.

When you next open a bottle of dry white wine, sip it on its own to see what it tastes like (hopefully, pleasant, light and fruity). Now try a mouthful of some neutral food – some bread or a small piece of plainly cooked cold chicken – and try the wine again. It should taste almost exactly the same. Now (if you can bear it) suck a quarter of lemon, and try the wine again. It will suddenly taste dull and flabby. Now try something sweet, like a spoonful of chocolate mousse, and you'll find the wine turns thin and sour.

There are three ways wine and food can react:

■ they can clash horribly – like your white wine and lemon or chocolate;

■ they can co-exist pretty happily – if you try them together your wine should taste much the same as it did when you sipped it on its own, and so should your food;

■ they can fall madly in love – the food enhances the wine, the wine makes the food taste better.

As in real life, these intense love affairs are few and far between. Even if you give the most helpful guidelines, you can't always get it right. You can say, for instance, that x is generally wonderful with y, but it depends on the recipe, how you've cooked the dish, how long the wine has been hanging around in a cupboard – even what kind of a mood you're in. If you've just had a massive row with the love of your life, the most perfect coupling of food and wine won't taste right. Suffice it to say that the more you understand about the way wine and food react together, the more likely you are to get it right. And there will be occasions when it's just perfect.

How to get a harmonious match
What we aim for most of the time is finding wines and foods that are in harmony, and avoiding ones that clash horribly. To some extent this is a question of personal taste: if you really don't like red wine then there's no point in being told that claret and roast beef are the perfect combination. On the other hand, if you're cooking or ordering in a restaurant for other people, you have to take their likely preferences into account.

Two questions to ask

There are two key questions to ask yourself about a dish in order to decide which wine to serve with it:

How is the food cooked?

What is the dominant flavour on the plate?

Concentrating on the way a dish is cooked is more useful than focusing on the basic ingredient in it. You should aim to match light food with light wines and heavier, fuller-flavoured food with heavier wines (see Chapter 8 for information on wine styles).

Light dishes include food that is served raw, steamed, poached or microwaved. Heavy dishes include food that has been subject to more robust cooking methods such as frying, grilling and roasting, or which have a strongly flavoured or rich sauce.

But the cooking method is not quite enough to base a decision on. You could, for instance, have steamed fish (which should, in theory, be light) served with black bean sauce, which would make it heavy. Or a rack of lamb, quickly roasted, which would leave it pink and quite light. You also need to focus on the flavour of what you're eating – and you can find out how to do this in the next chapter.

CHAPTER 13

Focus on the Flavour

The dominant flavour in what you're eating is all-important. Take a simple roast chicken - easy enough to pair with wine. Either a light or medium-bodied red or white will do. But what if you serve the chicken in a creamy white wine and mushroom sauce? Or in a Provençal tomato and garlic-flavoured sauce? What if you cut it into strips for an oriental-style stir-fry, or serve it on skewers in a satay sauce? You'll want a different wine each time.

If you focus on the flavour of what you're eating rather than the main ingredient, you'll find choosing a wine a whole lot easier.

Ten common flavours - and the wines to match them

Meaty

Dishes in which the flavour of the meat rather than any sauce or seasoning is predominant: eg plainly grilled steak or chops, roasts, meaty casseroles like steak and kidney, or braised oxtail.

Wine matches:

Plainly grilled or roast meat is pretty flexible but tends to go best with a rich, smooth red like a Cabernet Sauvignon. Casseroles may need a beefier, gutsier red like a Shiraz. If you do want to drink white with a steak it needs to be a rich, fruity, oaky white like an Australian Chardonnay or Sémillon.

Fishy

Dishes in which the flavour of the fish rather than any sauce is

predominant: eg shellfish,
plainly grilled white
fish, poached salmon.

Wine matches:
Shellfish and simply prepared white fish are perfect with a crisp, dry
white like Muscadet or a Sauvignon. Salmon is a richer fish which
needs a fuller, rounder wine like classic white Burgundy or
Chardonnay.

Creamy

Fish, chicken or pasta with a creamy sauce.

Wine matches:
Wine goes well with creamy dishes but you
need a full, well-rounded white to match the
richness. Three wines beginning with C will do
the trick: Chardonnay (French rather than
Australian), Chenin Blanc and Champagne.
(Desserts with cream also lend themselves well to sweet wines – see
next chapter.)

Cheesy
By this I don't mean smelly socks but
dishes like fish, pork, chicken
or veal with a light cheese
sauce, pasta dishes, or the
classic meat and cheese dishes
like cannelloni, lasagne and
moussaka.

Wine matches:
Cooked cheese is rich and needs a wine with lots of body or
luscious juicy fruit to cut through. With fish dishes, try a strongly
flavoured dry Italian white wine like a Lugana, or a good quality
Soave. Italian reds like Valpolicella and Barbera also work well.

Tomatoey
You meet tomato in many of the classic dishes of the Mediterranean,

such as Provençal fish soups and stews, Chicken Basquaise, pizza, pasta and even simple French tomato salad.

Wine matches:
Tomatoes can cause problems with wine because of their high acidity, so don't waste your best wine on them. White wines don't generally work, though a dry rosé can be good with a light dish like tomato salad. With more robust dishes you could serve a smooth Italian red or a full-bodied southern French red – even with fish.

Garlicky

Here we're not talking about the odd clove of garlic which nowadays everyone adds to almost everything but a dish with a pronounced garlicky flavour, like Chicken Kiev or prawns with aïoli (garlic mayonnaise).

Wine matches:
Go for gutsy New World wines: New Zealand Sauvignon (for fish and shellfish), Australian Chardonnay (for chicken and pork) and Shiraz or Zinfandel for beef or lamb. Inexpensive Eastern European wines should also survive.

Sweet/sour

Chinese food and various oriental stir-fries are the obvious example, but there are quite a few other dishes nowadays which combine savoury and sweet.

Wine matches:
Sweet/sour dishes are best with a slightly spicy, aromatic, off-dry white wine, which is where wines from Germany and Alsace come into their own. A dish with a strong fruit flavour – for instance, a pork and apricot casserole – needs a fruity wine to complement it, like a rich, tropical Australian Chardonnay.

Hot and spicy

If there's one thing we like as much as garlic, it's chillies. Mexican,

Thai and Indian food are all spicy, so what do you serve with them?

Wine matches:
The 'rules' say that you can't pair wine with hot spicy food, but today's New World wines can take on a surprising amount of heat. Cabernet Sauvignon, for example, works well with most curries, short of a vindaloo, while New Zealand Sauvignon is excellent with hot, spicy Thai food.

Smokey
Smokey dishes are the awkward squad – ranging from the delicate flavour of smoked fish pâtés and smoked salmon to the robust, challenging flavours of chargrilled food and barbecue sauces.

> ### Wine buff's tip
> What can sometimes be a help in choosing a wine is to focus on the fruit. Apples, for instance, go well with pork, so a soft appley wine like Chenin Blanc or Austrian Grüner Veltliner can work too. Ham and pineapple is a classic combination - rich, pineappley Sémillon would go well with a roast gammon joint; while dishes that benefit from a squeeze of lemon will taste good with a light citrussy white like a French Bergerac.

Wine matches:
Apart from smoked mackerel (with which it's not really worth serving any wine), Sauvignon Blanc stands up quite well to smoked fish and is particularly good with smoked salmon. For a barbecue, go for big, fruity reds or whites, but not ones with too much oak (see Chapter 20).

Sharp/tangy
Sharp or tangy dishes are ones in which vinegar or lemon predominate, such as salads and lemon-flavoured sauces.

Wine matches:
Potentially these flavours are wine killers. It's best to opt for dry, crisp, lemony, earthy whites with not too much rich fruit – Sauvignon rather than Chardonnay.

What if I have more than one of these flavours on the plate?

That's more than possible. You could have a hot spicy chilli with a sharply dressed salad, or plain roast lamb accompanied by a garlicky potato and cheese gratin and ratatouille.

The answer is to match the wine to the weightiest flavour. In the first case, that would probably be the chilli; in the second, you'd need to choose a gutsier wine than you might have picked with the lamb alone, to cope with the rich garlicky cheese and ratatouille (a southern French Corbières or Minervois rather than a light claret).

Food clashes

There are some foods which really don't do a great deal for wine – most experts rule out eggs, chocolate, artichokes and asparagus. You can in fact find wines to go (or at least not clash) with all of these things, but frankly, how often do we all down a glass with our bacon and egg or eat artichokes and asparagus?

If you want to be kind to the wine you're drinking, the answer is to avoid extremes of taste and temperature: foods that are very hot and spicy or very cold like ice creams and sorbets, or foods that are very salty, sour or sweet.

Watch out for the effect of:

■ A squeeze of lemon
■ Vinegary or strongly flavoured chutneys and relishes
■ Raw onion or garlic
■ Sharp salad dressings
■ Oily flavours and textures – eg fish such as anchovies, herring, mackerel and sardines.

CHAPTER 14

Wine with Cheese and Desserts

So far we've been looking at wines you would drink with starters and main courses, as normally these would be the items you'd match a bottle to. But what about cheese and puddings? Can you drink the same sort of wines with them?

Wine with cheese

Wine and cheese is supposed to be the perfect combination of food and wine. But in practice, it's rather more tricky than it might seem. Again, the idea stems from a time when the cheeseboard was pretty plain and simple and the wine you were drinking was likely to be a hefty tannic Bordeaux. There wasn't such a thing as Stilton with apricots, or garlic Roule, or a wine like Australian Chardonnay.

In fact, white wines often go very well with cheese, which isn't so surprising when you think how well cheese goes with fruit or a sweet chutney – think of that traditional North Country combination of apple pie and cheese.

What counts in a cheese and wine match is how strong the cheese is, and that's usually determined by how mature it is. Cheddar, for instance, can be quite mild; but it can also be bitingly sharp. Brie can be mild and chalky or ripe and runny. The more mature the cheese, the more powerful the wine you should drink with it.

When you plan a cheeseboard, try to find cheeses that are compatible with the same wine.

A quick cheese and wine guide

Soft, mild cheeses – eg Brie and Camembert, Bel Paese.
A light red works well: a Beaujolais if the cheese is very mild, a fruity Côtes du Rhône, Valpolicella or Merlot if it is a bit more mature.

Hard cheeses – eg the classic English cheeses like Cheddar, Cheshire, Lancashire and Caerphilly.
If the cheese is mild, a light fruity red or even a white wine will work (provided it isn't too acidic). A full oaky Chardonnay is excellent with mature Cheddar, and with a cheese that has some sweetness of its own like Stilton with apricots. But a big gutsy red like a Shiraz or a Chianti will also work well.

Hard waxy cheeses – eg Gruyère, Emmenthal, Jarlsberg.
Milder cheeses like Jarlsberg are fairly flexible. With the more pronounced, intense flavour of Gruyère you'd be better off with a Gewürztraminer or an oaky red wine with a touch of sweetness.

Blue cheeses – eg Stilton, Danish blue, Gorgonzola, Roquefort.
Strong blue cheeses aren't ideal with red wine but they need something powerful. The classic French combination is Roquefort and Sauternes, but you could try a less expensive sweet wine like an Auslese or a Muscat. Port is the traditional partner for Stilton, but make it tawny rather than ruby or late bottled vintage. A rich amontillado sherry is even better.

Strong, smelly cheeses – eg Pont l'Évêque, Munster.
These tend to be cheeses that you love or loathe – either way they're not too kind to wine. A big Aussie Shiraz or a spicy Alsace

Gewürztraminer are the safest bets.

Goats' cheese
Goats' cheese has a strange, almost bitter flavour that for some reason goes very well with a Sauvignon Blanc. Try it and see.

Smoked cheeses
These can also be tricky. Try a semi-sweet white like a Morio Muskat.

Cheeses with added flavours – eg garlic and herbs, peppercorns, walnuts.
Although most of these cheeses are basically soft and mild, adding an extra ingredient like garlic or pepper makes them quite potent. A really fresh young zippy red like a Hungarian Merlot can just about cope. With a nutty cheese, try an amontillado sherry.

Wine buff's tip

If you want to drink wine with your cheese, you're better off serving it French-style after the main course - unless you're drinking a dessert wine, in which case you could have a slice of Stilton or other blue cheeses to follow.

Desserts

Main-course wines don't really go with desserts so we don't often get round to drinking a wine with our pudding. This is a huge shame as there are some wonderful dessert wines (see Chapter 10), many of which are quite inexpensive.

There are two principles to remember about matching wines to desserts:

They should be sweeter than the dessert they accompany. A wine that is less sweet will taste sour by comparison.

They should match the pudding weight for weight. A light wine with a light pudding, a heavier wine for a richer, sweeter pudding.

A quick wine and dessert guide

Fruity desserts
Most desserts are fruity so the choice of wine depends on the kind of fruit:

Apples and pears are not too sweet or too sour and will generally go with most light sweet wines.

Lemon-flavoured puddings tend to be tart. Try a soft, honeyed sparkler like Clairette de Die.

Peaches and nectarines are perfect with wine: classic with an off-dry Champagne.

Red fruits like strawberries can be quite acidic: a light, soft, sweet fizz like a Moscato d'Asti or Asti Spumante goes well.

Creamy desserts - eg crème brûlée, tiramisu.
With a rich creamy dessert you need a sweet wine with some weight, like a Muscat de Beaumes-de-Venise.

Wine buff's tip

Pouring cream on fruit or adding it in a mousse will cut the acidity of the fruit and make the dessert richer, so you will need a sweeter wine.

Cheesecakes
Can be very rich so don't put too sweet a wine with them (unless they have a very sweet fruit topping). Try a Moscatel de Valencia.

Chocolatey desserts
Chocolate is a wine lover's nightmare. The only wine I've found to go perfectly is an extraordinary Californian sweet red wine called Elysium, though Orange Muscat is pretty good with rich dark chocolate desserts.

Sweet and sticky desserts - eg pecan pie, sticky toffee pudding, treacle tart.

This type of dessert needs a mega-sweet wine like an Australian Liqueur Muscat or a late harvest Riesling. Strictly for the sweet-toothed.

Ice cream

Generally to be avoided with wine, but Liqueur Muscat is magic with real vanilla or any kind of toffee crunch ice cream.

CHAPTER 15

Matching Food to Wine

Most of the time we match wine to food, but there are times when somebody gives you (or you buy yourself) a special bottle and you want the wine to be the star.

One option, of course, is not to eat anything at all with it and simply enjoy it on its own. That would be fine with light wines like Champagne, Sauvignon or Riesling, which you can sip as an aperitif.

With first-class Burgundy, Bordeaux or a sweet Sauternes that isn't really an option – and you're also likely to want to drink something else first. Whatever it is – and it oughtn't to be too overpowering – there shouldn't be a lot of it, otherwise you and everyone else will have run out of steam by the time the Great Bottle arrives on the table.

So far as food is concerned, the golden rule is to keep it simple. Use first-class ingredients and don't go overboard on the trimmings. This is the time to cook a good fillet steak, a simply roasted pheasant or duck, or a fabulous piece of grilled or baked fish. Basically, a good bottle of wine is a treat and a great opportunity to be unashamedly indulgent about the food.

Good matches for great wines

Champagne – oysters, smoked salmon, lobster, fish or light meat in creamy sauces.

White Burgundy – similar, but don't waste it on smoked salmon. Chablis is traditional for oysters.

An expensive Sauvignon from the Loire (Pouilly-Fumé or Sancerre) - a French-style *plateau des fruits de mer* (a selection of fresh shellfish), dressed crab, smoked salmon.

Red Burgundy – roast pheasant or other game.

Red Bordeaux – fillet steak, plainly roasted ribs of beef, saddle of lamb.

CHAPTER 16

Cooking with Wine

Wine has never played a major part in British cooking. Not ever having had vast quantities of cheap wine, adding wine to a dish always seemed rather an extravagance instead of an everyday practice as in France and Italy.

But now that we've become a nation of wine drinkers it's quite normal to have a half-empty bottle or two hanging around in the kitchen. And rather than waste it, it's much better to add it to food.

Cook with decent wine

Using wine in cooking is a bit like using a computer. If you put rubbish in, you get rubbish out. The dregs of a wine that has been hanging around since last Christmas aren't going to do anything for your cooking.

That said, inexpensive everyday drinking wine will do wonders. And it doesn't matter a lot whether it's red or white (as long as it's not too sweet). The main difference is the colour it gives the dish, so you would be unlikely to put red wine into a fish dish very often.

What happens to wine when you cook it is that it reduces and gives an intensity and depth of flavour to a dish, but it doesn't taste especially alcoholic. Even a spoonful or two added to an everyday dish like Spaghetti Bolognese will take it into the luxury league.

There are three main ways you can use wine in food:

■ **As an instant gravy.** A little wine added to the pan in which you have cooked a steak or chops, to release all the delicious crusty bits in the pan, makes a brilliant instant gravy.

■ **In a sauce.** Many of the classic French sauces have wine in them. It cuts the richness of a light creamy sauce, softens the edges of a tomato sauce, and miraculously transforms other quite humdrum ingredients into something special.

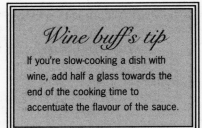

Wine buff's tip

If you're slow-cooking a dish with wine, add half a glass towards the end of the cooking time to accentuate the flavour of the sauce.

■ **In a slow braised casserole or stew.** Here far more wine is used to produce an intense, richly flavoured sauce that permeates right through the meat. Often the meat is marinated in the same wine first.

Six great French dishes made with wine

Soupe à l'oignon (onion soup cooked with dry white wine)
Soupe de pêcheurs (a Provençal fish soup, cooked with white wine)
Moules marinières (mussels cooked with white wine)
Coq au vin (chicken in red wine)
Entrecote Bordelaise (steak with red wine sauce)
Boeuf Bourguignon (beef cooked in Burgundy)

If you use a particular wine to make a great classic recipe such as Boeuf Bourguignon, it makes sense to drink the same type of wine with the finished dish.

Sweet dishes with wine

As well as savoury dishes, wine can be used in all kinds of sweet dishes:
■ you can poach pears in a syrup made with red wine, or peaches in white wine
■ you can soak strawberries in red wine for half an hour before serving them
■ you can use marsala to make a classic Italian zabaglione.

PS Don't forget sherry

Much maligned sherry is also a wonderful cooking aid. It keeps well, and because it's fortified with brandy you only need a little to add flavour to a dish. You can use it to zip up an onion soup or rich stew, or to add depth to a sauce; you can add it to Chinese cooking instead of rice wine and, so long as it's sweet, use it to make a good old-fashioned sherry trifle.

CHAPTER 17

Ordering Wine in a Restaurant

Even if you know a fair bit about
wine (and by now you do) ordering it in a
restaurant can still be off-putting. There are
still far too many restaurants that seem to
enjoy making the whole
experience as mystifying as
possible, with some snooty wine
waiter producing a gigantic
leatherbound wine list, then
hovering over your shoulder while
you try to wade through it.

There are enlightened
restaurants that offer a short, well-
chosen list and plenty of half
bottles and wines by the glass, but
there are also many that never get
beyond a load of dreary, over-priced French classics.

Armed with all your new-found knowledge, you should in fact be
able to work your way round the list and find a wine to match what
you're eating. But you still don't know what the particular bottle the
restaurant stocks tastes like - or exactly how the chef has cooked the
dish. So, rule number one is...

Don't be afraid to ask

It's not showing your ignorance to ask the restaurant manager or
wine waiter about the wine - it's common sense. Unless you're a
regular, you won't have tasted the wine with the food on the menu.
He has, or certainly should have done. Wine waiters are there to tell

you about the wines on their list; it's what the restaurant's paying them for. And in fact it makes their job more interesting; just fetching and carrying the wine you order is pretty boring.

If you ask for a recommendation, they should ask you what type of wine you like: white, red, lighter or more full-bodied? If they don't, make your preferences clear so they don't suggest a wine you won't enjoy.

What if they recommend a wine I can't afford?

The easiest way to avoid this situation is to give them an indication of how much you want to pay; but that may not be easy if you're with guests or business acquaintances. You can get round the problem by saying, 'I thought we might have the x or y' (naming two wines within your price bracket) – 'which do you suggest?'

If you can't find anyone in the restaurant who knows anything about the wine – and it can and does happen – look through the list for the following:

Wines listed by the name of the grape – eg Chardonnay, Sauvignon, Cabernet Sauvignon, Merlot (see Chapters 1 and 6).

Well known branded wines – they may not be the most exciting wines on the list but they should be a safe bet (see Chapter 7).

New World wines – generally better value in restaurants than a well known French or Italian wine, unless you know the restaurant well and the wine waiter recommends it.

Should I try the house wine?

A good restaurant with a reputation to protect isn't going to sell a bad house wine, but they aren't always the value for money they appear. It may be something the restaurant owner has picked up for five francs a litre from a warehouse in Calais and is selling for ten times the price. As a general rule, it's better to look for a wine with a name and a vintage, preferably a recent one.

What if everyone orders different dishes?

This is the real nightmare about picking wine in restaurants (and why it's handy to be able to off-load the responsibility to the wine waiter, if you can). If half the party are having meat and the other half fish, the usual solution is to have two bottles – usually a white with the starter and a red with the main course for those who are eating a meaty or strongly flavoured dish.

If everyone is ordering food with totally different flavours the only solution is to order a full-bodied, food-friendly wine that will stand up to a wide spectrum of flavours: the two safest bets being Chardonnay and Merlot. They may not be great with everyone's dish but they should please most people.

If you are dining by yourself, or there are just two of you, the ideal solution is to order wine by the glass. If that option is not available, two half bottles are generally more flexible than one bottle right through the meal.

Wine buff's tip

There are some wine-producing areas that offer particularly good value for money because they are less well known. The wines from Alsace in France (such as Pinot Blanc, Pinot Gris, Riesling and Gewürztraminer) are generally great with food, and you seldom find a bad one. Other lesser known wines from France (like *vin de pays* wines), Italy (especially from the south), Portugal and Spain are also good value because restaurateurs believe they don't carry the same prestige as their better known counterparts.

How many bottles should I order?

Not too many to start with – you can always order another one if need be. One bottle (or two half bottles) should serve two to three people through a meal, two bottles should be enough for up to five, and three bottles for six to eight.

Tasting the wine

Once you've ordered your wine, you need to taste it. When the waiter presents the bottle to you, check the label to see that it's what you ordered – looking out particularly for the year and the producer. Then simply follow the tasting guidelines in Chapter 3.

When you smell the wine you should be able to tell if there's something seriously wrong with it. If it's vinegary or sulphurous, tell the waiter straightaway and get him to check it. He should replace it at this stage without question.

It can be slightly more tricky if you simply think it's not a very good wine, or not what you expected. Use common sense here. If the wine is sour-tasting or cabbagey (usually a white) or dried out and lacking in fruit (usually a red), point this out. Even if you've selected the cheapest wine on the list, you're entitled to expect it to be fresh and fruity.

An unexpected taste is harder to deal with. If you have made it clear what kind of wine you like and the waiter has recommended one to you, then you are entitled to send it back if it doesn't fit the bill. If you picked the wine and it's not what you expected, you're on less strong ground. If there's nothing actually wrong with it, you just have to put it down to experience.

Finally, don't be afraid to ask the waiter to chill the wine a little longer if it's not cold enough.

Restaurant mark-ups

One thing that always causes a good deal of grief is the price of wines in restaurants. Generally you will find them at least twice the price you will in the shops, but before you get hot under the collar, remember the restaurant has to pay for storage, glasses and the wages of whoever pours it for you (plus all their other overheads). Depending on where the restaurant is you should be able to get a house wine for around £8-10 a bottle, a more than acceptable named wine for £10-15, and a seriously good wine for £15-20. Any more than this and your restaurant's probably overcharging.

PART V

*E*ntertaining

———

CHAPTER 18

Sit-down Meals

Entertaining is much more relaxed and informal these days. Basically, it's about having friends round; the occasion can range from a spontaneous get-together over a takeaway to the most meticulously planned dinner party.

What these occasions have in common is that they're sit-down meals, rather than parties, and the food generally arrives in courses. With parties, which we'll look at in the next chapter, not only do you often have to stand up (or balance your food perilously on your knee) but there tends to be a range of dishes, which poses its own problems for food-and-wine matching.

Sit-down meals
When you plan a meal a number of factors determine what you decide to give your guests to eat. The same goes for the wine:

the occasion – whether you're simply having friends or family round, or have something special to celebrate. Asking a couple of neighbours over to share a takeaway is obviously different from cooking a special meal to celebrate your grandparents' golden wedding anniversary;

your guests – how adventurous they are about food and wine, and how well you know them. An experiment from your new Thai cookbook with friends who are mad about hot, spicy food is going to be different from inviting the boss and his wife (or her husband) round for the first time;

the time of year – whether it's spring, summer, autumn or winter; or unseasonably hot or cold. By and large, you're going to want lighter food and wines in the summer and hot weather; more warming, robust food and wine in the winter and when it's cold;

your budget – whether you're splashing out or trying to put the meal together as inexpensively as possible;

and last, but not least, **your own preferences** – there's no point in serving up food or wine that you personally detest.

Wine as an aperitif

With most occasions, you're likely to want to serve your guests a drink before the meal – what the French call an *aperitif*. While you always get some diehard who won't be satisfied unless you offer them a gin and tonic or a pint of lager, most people are more than happy if you serve them a glass of wine.

The advantage so far as you're concerned is that it cuts the cost quite substantially. You don't have to buy a whole load of other drinks and the wine you start with can carry you through the first course of the meal. Generally, a dry white wine or a light fortified wine like sherry fits the bill better than red, though the golden rule is that it should be cold and it shouldn't be too heavy. (Although the French often drink a chilled glass of sweet Muscat wine before a meal, it's not to everyone's taste.)

Remember, if you have some kind of nibbles with your drink, that they can affect the wine you're drinking. Nuts and crisps are pretty neutral, but start to lay out spicy snacks or more substantial nibbles along the lines of party food and you'll need to choose rather more carefully.

Good aperitif wines

■ Crisp, dry, fruity whites like a Sauvignon or a more flowery German Riesling.
■ Chilled fino sherry (which will cope with strongly flavoured nibbles).
■ An inexpensive sparkling wine – or if you are celebrating, Champagne.

How much wine do I need to buy?

Again, it depends on your guests and the occasion, but two glasses a head is a reasonably reliable rule of thumb for the meal itself (allow a little extra if you're having wine as an aperitif, or changing wines through the meal).

For 2-3 people, allow one bottle
For 4-6 people, two bottles
For 7-9 people, three bottles
And for 10-12 people, four bottles.

Informal entertaining: one-wine meals

Now we've all got the continental habit of drinking wine with our meals, the idea of buying a bottle to enjoy with the Sunday lunch or the Saturday-night Chinese takeaway isn't as outlandish as it would have seemed even ten years ago. The crucial thing about informal entertaining is that the wine doesn't have to be expensive; you can generally find a bottle that fits the bill for under £3.

For most informal occasions it's enough to have one type of wine, even if the numbers dictate you might need a couple of bottles of it. (It's better to stick to the same wine than top up half-empty glasses with a different one.) For some examples, look at the suggestions below. For more general advice, check Chapter 13.

Four wines to drink with takeaways:

Chinese – Chinese food goes well with an off-dry white. Try an inexpensive German Riesling.

Curry – A robust fruity red such as an Australian Cabernet Sauvignon or Shiraz should be able to cope with most curries, except a vindaloo. If you prefer white, stick to German.

Fish and chips – You want a white wine that acts like a squeeze of lemon juice. An inexpensive Sauvignon or white Portuguese Bairrada would do.

Pizza – Light, juicy Italian reds go perfectly with tomato and cheese. Pick a Valpolicella or an Italian Merlot.

Other one-wine meals

A traditional Sunday lunch
Menu: Roast beef and Yorkshire pudding.
Roast beef is probably the easiest dish in the world to match as it will go with almost any full-bodied red wine. Claret (red Bordeaux) is traditional and works perfectly.

A midweek pasta supper for two
Menu: Tagliatelle with cream, ham and mushrooms.
White would probably be better than red with this dish. An Italian or Hungarian Chardonnay would work well (but don't go for the oaky Australian style).

A Mexican supper for four
Menu: Guacamole, fresh tomato salsa and tortilla chips.
Chille con carne with rice and a mixed salad.
In theory this menu with its heat, spice and raw onion is fraught with problems for the wine drinker. A Chilean or Australian Cabernet Sauvignon could take it.

A Greek summer supper for eight
Menu: Assorted Greek dips and pitta bread, kebabs, rice and mixed Greek salad.
Another troublesome menu that needs a flavoursome wine to cope. Good Greek wines are few and far between, so unless you are a retsina addict, hop across to next-door Bulgaria and go for one of the new young fruity (rather than traditional oaky) reds.

A Thai meal for four
Menu: Thai fish cakes, Thai-style chicken curry.
Thai food is delicious but hot, so tricky from a wine point of view. A well-chilled New Zealand or South African Sauvignon Blanc would have the same effect as a glass of ice-cold lager.

More formal entertaining: two- or three-wine meals

Dinner parties and more formal lunches are usually carefully planned three-course affairs in which the food is the centrepiece, so you don't want the wine to let you down. That said, there's generally no need to spend over £5 a bottle, even if you're wanting to impress.

What you may, however, want to do is to match a wine to each course – or at least to two courses – serving, for example, one wine before the meal and with the first course, and another with the main course. Or you could serve a wine that would take you through the starter and main course, and serve another wine with the dessert. Which way you play it depends on your particular culinary talents. If you're a whizz at desserts, you might like to serve a wine to show off your masterpiece.

If you're being serious about the food, try to avoid having too many flavours on the plate otherwise your wine simply won't be able to cope. Offering, for instance, your guests a choice of fruit salad, creamy pavlova and chocolate gâteau may delight the sweet-toothed, but you might as well forget the wine.

Four seasonal menus

All the ingredients for the suggested menus which follow can be obtained from good supermarkets, and the recipes for the various dishes can be found in many popular cookery books and magazines.

An Easter family lunch
Menu: Roast lamb with spring vegetables. Lemon tart.
Even though it's Easter it's a family occasion, so play the wine on the conservative side. Red would be nicer than white with lamb, but as it's spring don't make it too heavy. If you feel like splashing out a good Burgundy would be perfect, otherwise go for a light, inexpensive Rioja. You might like to have a glass of inexpensive sparkling wine first (if you were serving Rioja you could stick to Spanish and make it Cava). Or you could serve a glass of soft, sweet, sparkling Moscato d'Asti with the lemon tart.

A Mediterranean summer supper

Menu: Grilled vegetables. Chargrilled chicken with couscous and mixed green salad. Baked peaches with mascarpone cheese (a very rich cream cheese).

Stick to your Mediterranean theme and pick your wines from the South of France. A full-bodied but very dry white like a Terret (or Spanish Rueda) would start the meal off well. Follow it with a big gutsy red Fitou, Corbières or Minervois, which would cope with the strong flavours of the chicken. If you wanted a glass of wine with the dessert, you could buy a half bottle of inexpensive French Muscat.

An autumn dinner party for six

Menu: A warm salad with pancetta (Italian-style bacon) and chicken livers. Roast pheasant with a potato and celeriac purée. Pear and almond tart.

A quality German Riesling would be a good aperitif and work well with the first course. Red Burgundy is a classic with game, but if you wanted to fool your friends you could always decant a bottle of Romanian Pinot Noir. With the pear and almond tart you could serve a glass of Moscatel de Valencia.

A mid-winter dinner party for six

Menu: Mussel and saffron soup. Daube of beef. Crème brûlée and caramelised oranges.

This meal starts rich and ends rich. You'd be better to have a glass of good dry Spanish amontillado sherry before the meal, and skip wine with the soup. With the daube, a rich beef stew, you could serve a traditional Portuguese Garrafeira wine. A noble late harvest sweet Riesling would be good with the pud.

Bringing a bottle

If you're the guest rather than the host, you might feel you would like (or in the case of close friends or family, even be asked) to bring along a bottle. If you're asked, then check what the food is going to be and pick your bottle accordingly. If you take along a bottle on spec, it's better to assume that your hosts will have laid on wine already and to take something slightly more unusual. A bottle of sparkling wine is always welcome (as you have already discovered in Chapter 9, it doesn't have to be an expensive one), a dessert wine would be a good choice, or if it's winter, why not take along a half bottle of sherry or port.

Vegetarian entertaining

Just because your guests are vegetarian doesn't mean they won't enjoy wine – as you will know if you're a vegetarian yourself. Some vegetarians, however, do have objections to wines that are produced in the normal commercial way, in the same way as they are concerned about the food they eat. If you are entertaining someone who feels strongly about the issue, you can buy organic wines which are approved by a recognised authority.

So far as matching wines to food are concerned, exactly the same rules apply – concentrate on the flavour of what you're cooking. Here's an example:

A vegetarian dinner for six
Menu: Roasted red peppers with olive oil. Spinach and cheese roulade. Summer fruit sorbets.
Roasted red peppers are a strong-flavoured starter which would work well with a smooth, juicy Italian red like Primitivo. You could carry on drinking the same wine with the main course. You might well want a glass of white wine before the meal. A refreshing Sauvignon Blanc would be ideal.

Special celebrations

For special celebrations you want to produce the very best food you can – and the best wines too. That doesn't necessarily mean complicated recipes or hugely expensive bottles, but it does mean first-class ingredients and wines that match them perfectly. Champagne is a natural for celebrations but it doesn't come cheap, so build the meal around it rather than thinking of the food first. In fact, it's surprisingly versatile – so long as you avoid really strong spicy or garlicky flavours.

A romantic dinner for two

Menu: A salad of king prawns. Pan-seared scallops with oriental stir-fried greens. Passion fruit sorbet.

Although this is an intensely flavoured menu, it is one that would suit a good Champagne (as long as you're not too heavy on the soy sauce).

Bollinger would be perfect, but unless this is the night you plan the proposal, you might want to settle for a less expensive (but still full-flavoured) Champagne. Skip a dessert wine, unless you want to spend the rest of the evening asleep.

A birthday or anniversary dinner for two

Menu: Smoked salmon parcels. Seafood kebabs with saffron rice. Individual fruit tartlets.

Again, this menu is rich but you could drink Champagne with it. A good alternative would be half a bottle of Champagne with the first course, then half a bottle of good quality Chardonnay. If you felt like pushing the boat out you could have a glass of Sauternes with the dessert.

A golden wedding anniversary dinner for eight

Menu: Melon, tomato and cucumber salad. Chicken in a cream and mushroom sauce. Chocolate and hazelnut meringue gâteau. An English cheeseboard.

This rather more traditional menu reflects the fact that older people generally prefer lighter and less strongly flavoured food. They also tend to prefer rather sweeter wines – and fewer of them. If you served a soft Italian sparkler like a Moscato or Asti Spumante before the meal, you could skip wine with the starter and move on to a medium-dry white wine which would match the chicken's creamy sauce. A *demi-sec* Vouvray would be perfect. (You could also provide a bottle of light Loire red wine as an alternative.) Forget wine with the pudding and offer a glass of port with the cheeseboard.

CHAPTER 19

Parties and Celebrations

Once parties used to be an excuse to serve up the roughest, cheapest wine you could lay your hands on. Nowadays good wine is so inexpensive – and inexpensive wine so good – that there's really no excuse for not offering something drinkable.

It still isn't (or shouldn't be) a question of picking up any wine that happens to be on special offer. Even though it's a party, not just any wine will do.

Four things to remember about party drinking

Choose light but fruity wines.
Party food generally contains a huge range of conflicting flavours which are going to be hard on any wine you pick. Nowadays many of those flavours will be spicy, which would normally call for quite robust, full-flavoured wines. But there's something about the party situation – whether it's because people are drinking all evening or because it can get so hot – that calls for lighter wines than you would normally choose. But they still need to be fruity to stand up to the food.

Be prepared to spend more on your white wine than on your red.
Inexpensive red wines are generally pretty palatable. But white wines often need to be chilled to taste good. Even if you get yourself really well organised (see tips on cooling large quantities of wine below), you're unlikely to be able to serve your white wine as cold as you would for a dinner party, and some may have to be drunk at room temperature. Just buying a slightly better quality white can pay dividends.

123

You don't have to buy as much wine as you think you do.
The curious thing about parties is that the more people there are, the less they eat and drink per head. So while you would allow up to half a bottle per person for a small dinner party, one bottle between three should be ample for a large party. You can make both your food and wine go further by not offering too much choice. If people see several interesting looking bottles of wine, they're inclined to sample all of them. A choice of two or three different wines is quite sufficient.

Wine buff's tip

Someone is sure to spill red wine on your carpet. The slightly surprising solution is to immediately pour some dry white wine over the stain while it is still wet, then mop up. If you don't notice the stain until the next morning, there are commercial stain-removers for red wine.

Offer a no- and low-alcohol alternative.
While it's thoughtful to do this for a dinner party (and in any case there are usually soft drinks ready to hand), it's essential to cater for the non-drinkers and drivers at a party. Even the drinkers may appreciate a refreshing non-alcoholic drink during the course of the evening. (See Chapter 22.)

Which wines to choose

Parties are not the occasion to experiment with interesting wine and food combinations. Given the large numbers of people with varying tastes, you need to find a wine that is going to please the majority, so don't go for anything too rarified.

For cold food the basic choice should be:
a soft, fruity red (remember that lots of people don't like tannic wines) - a Hungarian or Italian Merlot would be perfect;
a fresh, dry, fruity white - a French country white like a Vin de Pays des Côtes de Gascogne or a South African Colombard or Chenin Blanc.

If you wanted to you could also provide an off-dry white like a

Hungarian country white or a dry Muscat, or even a German Riesling, in which case you could make your basic white even drier – such as an Italian Pinot Grigio or an inexpensive Sauvignon Blanc.

For hot food you can offer slightly more robust wines but still don't make them too oaky. An Australian or South African Chardonnay for the white and a fruity Australian or Chilean Cabernet Sauvignon for the red (which should cost you in the region of £3–4) would be ideal.

For a drinks party that is going to go on for just a couple of hours rather than the whole evening, an inexpensive sparkler is an excellent choice and goes well with most party nibbles. Remember to offer orange juice for an instant Bucks Fizz for those who want to dilute theirs.

Bottles or boxes?

Wine boxes seem like the perfect answer to party drinking – and in many ways they are. The only snag is they're tricky to chill. Most shops will sell bottles on a sale or return basis, so if you do order more than you want you can get your money back.

Party glasses

Few of us have enough glasses to cope with more than a dozen guests. Again, most shops will hire glasses – a far better option than paper cups.

Keeping party wine cold

This is the big problem with party drinking, particularly as the fridge is usually chock-a-block with party puds. The only practical answer is a couple of plastic buckets and a lot of ice. If you forget to stock up the freezer yourself you can buy large bags of ice in some wine shops, supermarkets and freezer centres.

Themed parties

If you are throwing a party with a theme and producing food to match, don't exclude the wine from the festivities. Here are some examples:

An Italian pasta and pizza party
A soft, easy drinking Italian red like Valpolicella is ideal. For the white, you could choose a crisp, dry white like a Soave or one of the newer fruitier wines from the south of Italy or Sicily.

A Spanish paella party
Inexpensive fruity red and white wines from La Mancha, Navarra or Valdepeñas.

A Tex-Mex evening
There are wines from Mexico but Chile is an easier hunting ground and produces wines that will stand up to spicy food. Try a Chilean Cabernet Sauvignon and Sauvignon Blanc.

An American Independence Day barbecue
Californian wines aren't the cheapest but if you want to stick to North America, go for a red Zinfandel and a white Sauvignon Blanc (or Fumé Blanc as they sometimes call it in the States). Otherwise, choose inexpensive Australian, Chilean or South African wines. (More on barbies in the next chapter.)

Wine and cheese parties

Wine and cheese aren't always the perfect partners they're made out to be. But if you pick your wine and cheese carefully (see Chapter 14) it can be a great success. The best way to tackle it is to match the wines and cheeses from a particular country. You could, for instance, have a Beaujolais Nouveau party when the wine is released in November and lay on lots of crusty bread and delicious creamy French cheeses (and a few hunks of pâté). Another novel idea, and one that would work very well, would be to offer a couple of English white wines with English farmhouse cheeses. Try it and see.

Celebration parties

For some of the celebrations mentioned in the last chapter, such as special birthdays and anniversaries, you'll want to throw a party rather than a sit-down meal. The same is true for weddings and christenings.

By and large, food that is served on these occasions tends to be plainer and simpler than what you would serve at an informal party, which makes it worth spending more on a good wine. (If you are serving serious wine try and avoid mixing styles of food which clash - for instance, a joint of rare roast beef and a dish of Mediterranean-style grilled vegetables with cold poached salmon and cucumber salad.)

Don't be embarrassed to serve a less expensive sparkler rather than Champagne. Sparklers are so good these days that your guests are really unlikely to be able to tell the difference, and may even prefer it to the real stuff!

Four kinds of fizz to serve at a party

A wedding reception - Champagne or a top quality Californian, Australian or New Zealand sparkler.

A summer christening tea - something light and semi-sweet like a Moscato Spumante or Prosecco that will go with sandwiches and cakes.

A drinks party to celebrate a silver or golden wedding anniversary - Champagne or a French Crémant de Bourgogne, Crémant d'Alsace or Blanquette de Limoux.

An engagement party or twenty-first - Spanish Cava or an inexpensive Australian sparkler.

CHAPTER 20

Outdoor Eating

Outdoor eating calls for strong, simple, vivid flavours, not for bringing out your most subtle and serious wine. Almost any inexpensive wine will taste twice as good if you drink it on a hot sunny day, but there are a few tips which will make the pleasure even greater.

Picnics

Wine immediately lifts a picnic into an occasion. If you have an easy quaffing country French red, even a chunk of bread and cheese tastes special (as the food-loving French know well).

But picnics are really when rosé comes into its own - better than white which never quite seems gutsy enough for a picnic. Always hard to fit into a sit-down meal (because people have such strong prejudices against it), rosé is absolutely perfect served well chilled out in the open air.

Choose one of the newer, drier rosés that have begun to appear over the past year or so (see Chapter 8). You can generally tell them by their darker colour, rather than the pale candy-pink that used to be so common, but check the back label too. Look out particularly for New World rosés and rosés made by the so-called 'flying winemakers'.

An inexpensive sparkling wine is fabulous on a picnic, though you must be able to drink it chilled. Warm fizz is no fun at all. And take a couple of real glasses - even Champagne doesn't taste great drunk out of a paper cup. And remember, your fizz is likely to get shaken up on the journey so open it extra carefully.

How to keep your wine cool

The big problem with picnics is how to keep your wine cool. The easiest way is to pop on one of those insulated 'Rapid Ice' jackets which will cool the bottle down and keep it cool for at least a couple of hours (see Chapter 5). Failing that, chill your bottle thoroughly overnight in the fridge and pop it into the cold bag with a couple of ice-packs.

If you're picking up a bottle on the way, you can buy it ready-chilled in some shops (either from the fridge or in a few shops from a chiller machine) but you'll probably have to settle for white rather than rosé. As a last resort you could try plunging the bottle into some nearby running water, but if it's cold enough to work it's probably too cold to have a picnic.

> *Wine buff's tip*
> Red wines can be surprisingly nice chilled too, so long as they're young and fruity.

Barbecues

With barbecues you're dealing with even stronger-flavoured foods than picnics. Never mind the more-or-less burnt burgers, bangers and chicken legs, you've probably laid on two or three different salads and some garlic bread so you need good gutsy wines to cope with it all.

What you don't need is even more smoke and oak, so avoid heavy, tannic, well-aged reds. The best wines to go for are ones with really upfront fruity flavours. Australian wines, particularly Chardonnay and Shiraz, are perfect for a barbie (as you'd expect), so are wines from South Africa such as Chenin Blanc and Pinotage. New Zealand Sauvignon Blanc, with its rich gooseberry flavour, is surprisingly good with meat and a natural with salads.

If you're catering for large numbers and don't want to spend that much, look for inexpensive fruity wines from Bulgaria, Hungary and Spain. Some of the newer varieties like Gamza (a terrifically fresh raspberryish red) are perfect for a barbecue or a picnic.

Keeping the wine cold

Follow the tips on cooling wines for parties (see previous chapter). If it's hot, you may need even more ice.

CHAPTER 21

Christmas and the New Year

Even if you only buy a couple of bottles of wine a year, Christmas is the one time everyone wants to celebrate. But like other special occasions, we want to get it right, so it pays to do a bit of forward planning.

These days, the Christmas and New Year holidays tend to last a good week, so it's not only the Christmas meal you need to plan for. You might want to throw an unplanned party, or invite the neighbours round for mince pies and a glass of mulled wine, or you might just get thoroughly sick and tired of turkey and long for something spicy.

The six basic bottles you need for Christmas drinking

Half a dozen different kinds of wine will see you through Christmas and the New Year. That may sound a lot but they don't have to be expensive (see the budget sections below) and they'll keep for a few months if you don't drink them all.

Wines for the Christmas meal. For Christmas dinner itself you need a choice of red and white. If you're having the traditional turkey, remember your wine has to cope with all the trimmings like spicy stuffing, cranberry sauce and roast potatoes. That means it should be upfront and fruity. For the white, I'd be inclined to go for a Chardonnay, for the red a Rhône wine or an Australian Shiraz. The same wines would work if you're having pork, but for beef I'd be inclined to replace the Shiraz with a Cabernet Sauvignon or claret. Goose or duck are a touch trickier because they're more fatty. I'd pick a German or Alsace Riesling as the white, and a good juicy Italian red.

A celebration sparkler. Whenever you have it - on Christmas morning, before Christmas dinner or on New Year's Eve to see the New Year in - you should have a bottle of fizz. It doesn't have to be Champagne. Nowadays there's a sparkling wine to suit every pocket.

Something sweet and sticky. The traditional Christmas wine is port, and that may be your choice for the festivities. But a half bottle of a luscious, sweet dessert wine is heaven with the Christmas pud - and rather lighter at the end of a long, heavy meal. Or you could buy a bottle of really good sherry.

Party or stand-by wines. You need a couple of inexpensive, food-friendly wines that will suit every occasion: a light, fresh easy drinking white and a robust fruity red that can cope with everything from casseroles to spicy food, and even being turned into mulled wine. This is the time when a couple of wine boxes can really come in handy.

You can fit this formula into whatever budget you have.

Up to £30

Christmas dinner
Plan to spend £3.99 a bottle for a red and a white wine to go with your Christmas meal. New World wines provide good value at this price   £7.98

Sparkler
Allow up to £4.99 for an Australian sparkler or Spanish Cava if your taste is dry, or a Moscato or Asti Spumante if you prefer a sweeter wine   £4.99

Sweet wine
A half bottle of light, sweet Moscatel de Valencia or French

Muscat for your Christmas pudding   £2.99

Party wines
Look to Eastern Europe for value. You should be able to find
a fresh zingy white and fruity red for under £2.99 a bottle.
Four bottles will come to £11.96, or less if you take
advantage of seasonal special offers   £11.96

                                          Total £27.92

Up to £50

Christmas dinner
Up your budget to £4.99 a bottle and choose good quality
red and white wines from the New World or the French
Pays d'Oc   £9.98

Sparkler
A cheaper Champagne or one of the excellent New World
Champagne taste-alikes   £8.99

Sweet wine
A half bottle of port, Sauternes, or a wickedly sweet Australian
'sticky'   £6.99

Party wines
The easiest thing is to lay in a couple of wine boxes. You
should be able to find a three-litre box (which holds four
standard bottles) for £11.99 or under. Look for a familiar
grape variety like Cabernet Sauvignon rather than just red
or white   £23.98

                                          Total £49.94

Christmas dinner

If you are prepared to spend a bit more on your wine for this special occasion, it's hard to beat the French classics. A white Burgundy (which after all is Chardonnay) and a lesser known Rhône wine like Crozes-Hermitage or Lirac (which are cheaper than the better known Châteauneuf-du-Pape) would be excellent. £15 should cover the two   **£15.00**

Sparkler

You could either buy a really good bottle of Champagne or, if you had larger numbers to cater for, two bottles of a top quality sparkler. Allow up to £20   **£20.00**

Sweet wine

Port has come down substantially in price recently and there are some excellent bargains around. Allow up to £12 for a good bottle. Short of vintage port, an aged tawny or a single Quinta port would be best   **£12.00**

Party wines

If the budget will run to it, sparkling wine is the ideal thing for a Christmas drinks party. Allow, say, five bottles at £6.99 (which would be enough for 15-20 people)   **£34.95**

You might also want a couple of bottles to drink with other meals over the holiday period. Two bottles each of an inexpensive Sauvignon and Cabernet Sauvignon (up to £3.99) should fit the bill   **£15.96**

Total £97.91

Mulled wine

There's nothing nicer than a glass of mulled wine and a minced pie to kick off the Christmas festivities, and it's simplicity itself to make.

If you've got a bottle of red wine to hand use that, otherwise keep an eye open for inexpensive wines on special offer.

Traditional mulled wine

1 bottle, full-bodied red wine
½ pint (275ml) water
3oz (75g) caster sugar
4-6 cloves
Half a stick or ½tsp of ground cinnamon
Thinly pared rind of half a lemon

Method: Put the water and spices together in a large saucepan, heat and simmer for five minutes. Add the lemon rind and sugar, and stir gently until the sugar is dissolved. Pour in the wine, and heat till just below boiling point (it shouldn't boil or the alcohol will evaporate). Strain and serve while still hot in heat-proof glasses or mugs.

Wine buff's tip

Full-bodied reds tend to be better for mulled wine than light fruity reds. Look out for more traditional, rich, oaky wines from Spain, Portugal and Romania.

Wine as a gift

For the budding wine buff there's nothing nicer than being given a bottle of a wine they wouldn't normally buy themselves. Good quality claret, Burgundy and Champagne would obviously go down a bomb - but unfortunately they can cost a bomb too. For good value, it's hard to beat dessert wines, sherry and port (look through Chapters 10 and 11 for ideas).

Alternatively you might like to buy a slightly more exotic or unusual wine that they mightn't have tried.

Six unusual wines

Amarone della Valpolicella (*Ama-roh-nee*) – this is an extraordinary, rich, intense, almost sweet kind of Valpolicella that you could sip at the end of a meal instead of port.

Chateau Musar (*Shat-oh mews-ar*) – Lebanese wine sounds a joke but Chateau Musar, made by maverick winemaker Serge Hochar, is a superb, silky, voluptuous red that tastes like a first-class Burgundy, at a fraction of the price.

White Graves (*Grarv*) – a marvellously stylish, dry white wine from Bordeaux made from Sémillon and Sauvignon Blanc. If you have Chardonnay fatigue this is where to turn to.

Mas de Daumas Gassac (*Mass der do-mass ga-sack*) – a cult wine from the up-and-coming Languedoc in the South of France that has been compared with the best red Bordeaux. The white is highly regarded too.

Viognier (*vee-ony-ay*) – a rising star in the grape world, which makes extraordinarily delicate, delicious, almost perfumed white wines. The best, if you have money (around £20-30) to burn, is Condrieu – a great white wine from the Rhône region of France – but you can find less expensive wines (round about the £5 mark) from the Pays d'Oc.

Vouvray (*Voo-vray*) – a great underrated wine from the Loire region of France. Best known as a semi-sweet (*demi-sec*) white wine with delicious honeyed softness, but it also comes in excellent dry and sparkling versions.

CHAPTER 22

Healthy Drinking

No one can fail to be aware these days of the hazards of drinking too much. Fortunately, wine and the way it is drunk with meals is a much healthier option than spirits or high-strength lagers or ciders, which tend to be drunk on their own.

Current research, in fact, suggests that drinking moderate amounts of wine – and particularly red wine – can actually help against heart disease. Researchers recently found that the population of Toulouse in the South of France had a quarter the number of heart attacks – despite a diet high in rich and fatty food – than the population of Belfast or Glasgow. And they regularly drink red wine.

Nevertheless, it pays to be aware of how much alcohol you may be drinking, and how much you can drink without putting yourself at risk.

Safe limits

The amount of alcohol recommended as a maximum by the Health Education Authority and other official bodies is expressed in units. The general guideline is 14 units for women and 21 for men, but it depends to some extent on height and body weight. A unit is roughly equivalent to a glass of table wine or a small glass of sherry or port.

In fact, the level of alcohol differs quite a lot between one wine and another. A light German wine, for example, at 7.5 per cent is almost half the alcohol level of a big oaky Chardonnay at 13 per cent. You can check the amount of alcohol (expressed as % vol) on the label, where it has to be stated by law. To help you work out how many units there are in the wine you're drinking, check up on the following table.

WINE			SHERRY	
% VOL	**UNITS PER GLASS** (125ML)		**% VOL**	**UNITS PER MEASURE** (50ML)
15.0	1.9		18.0	0.9
14.5	1.8		17.5	0.9
14.0	1.8			
13.5	1.7			
13.0	1.6			**PORT**
12.5	1.6			
12.0	1.5		**% VOL**	**UNITS PER MEASURE** (50ML)
11.5	1.4			
11.0	1.4		22.0	1.1
10.5	1.3		21.5	1.1
10.0	1.3		21.0	1.1
9.5	1.2		20.0	1.0
9.0	1.1			
8.5	1.1			
8.0	1.0			
7.5	0.9			
7.0	0.9			

Safe drinking tips

There are other sensible precautions to follow when you're drinking
wine – or any other kind of alcohol:

■ Drink just before or with a meal rather than between meals. Avoid
drinking on an empty stomach.

■ Don't drink to slake your thirst. Have a glass of water or another
soft drink before you start drinking, and in between alcoholic drinks,
if you're getting thirsty.

■ It's better to drink a moderate amount regularly than an excessive amount all in one go, even if you are still within your weekly limit.

■ Try to have a couple of alcohol-free days each week.

■ Never, of course, go over the limit when you're driving.

Low alcohol options

There may be various reasons why you wish to limit your intake but not avoid alcohol all together – for instance, when you're at a party and are driving home. The two ways you can do this are to go for a wine that is low in – or has no – alcohol, and by diluting a normal strength wine.

No- or low-alcohol wines

There are some wines that are very low in alcohol on the market, but they haven't really taken off. Not that surprising if you've ever tasted them: having wine without alcohol is a bit like having an egg without a yolk. If you want to try for yourself, be aware of the following descriptions:

■ A de-alcoholised or alcohol-free wine or beer is one that has no more than 0.5 per cent alcohol.

■ Low-alcohol wines can contain up to 1.2 per cent alcohol.

It's not until you get over the 5 per cent mark you begin to find wines that taste like wine. Many of the soft, sweetish Italian sparklers like Moscato D'Asti and Asti Spumante are between 5 and 7 per cent, while many white German wines are between 7 and 9 per cent.

Diluting wine

Diluting wine is quite normal among the French who will happily slosh a bit of water or a few ice cubes into their *vin rouge* when the weather is hot. (It's also how French children acquire a taste for wine.) Another pleasant summer tipple is a spritzer, a half-and-half mixture of white wine and soda.

You can also dilute sparkling and fortified wines. The best known and most glamourous is Buck's Fizz, a delicious combination of fresh orange juice and (traditionally) Champagne, though you can equally well use a less expensive sparkler. You can buy the mix ready-made, though making your own is much better. Even more exotic is a Bellini, a mixture of peach juice and Champagne. Either way you want about one part juice to three parts wine.

Ruby port often used to be diluted with lemonade and still makes a refreshing drink topped with ice cubes and lemon. And if you ever get given a bottle of white port, try drinking it Portuguese-style with tonic and ice.

CHAPTER 23

Starting a Cellar

The word cellar conjures up images of some huge, dusty, cobweb-festooned room which can only be reached down a long flight of ancient stone steps. A few wine cellars are like that, though unless you have some palatial pile in the country, I guess you're unlikely to have one. But cellar also means in winespeak simply a collection of different wines, and once you're interested in wine it's really the logical next step.

The point of having a collection is that it not only means that you always have a bottle to hand, but that you can buy wine you like when it is available and the price is right (wine, like any other product, goes out of stock). You can also buy wines young and keep them for a couple of years, or longer; though this tends only to benefit more expensive red and a few white wines (see Chapter 8) and is only worth doing if you really like the taste of old wine.

Having a cellar is a bit like having a freezer – and there can be similar drawbacks. It's all too easy to have some massive spree and buy a whole lot of stuff you later decide you don't really like or want. The big trap is buying wine by the case. You often get a small

 reduction per bottle for buying what is called an unmixed case, but unless you're buying for a party it's worth asking yourself whether you really want a dozen bottles of that particular wine. You may be better off buying what's called a mixed case – three bottles each of four different wines (or two each of six, or even, if you like to experiment, 12 different bottles).

The other problem is stock control. You need to store the bottles in such a way that the ones you ought to drink first are easily available at the front, and the ones you want to keep at the back. It's easy to forget what you've got (rather like having things tucked away at the bottom of the freezer) unless you keep a record somewhere. Traditionally, this would have been a cellar book but any old notebook will do. Just jot down the wines and the

date when you buy them and make a note of when you should drink them by (see notes on storing wine in Chapter 4).

Planning a cellar

If it's worth keeping wine at all, it's worth keeping wine you like. So never buy a whole lot of wine untried even if it's on what appears to be a fantastic special offer. Watch out for those special offers too. It may be the shop is selling off bottles that have reached the end of their shelf life – fine for immediate drinking but not so good for keeping. Or they may be bottles from a not terribly successful vintage which are simply not lasting as well as they should do. Don't be too ambitious. Aim for wines you plan to drink over the next couple of years rather than into the next century, and don't buy too many of them.

An inexpensive cellar

A useful, basic cellar could be made up as follows:

■ Six bottles each of your favourite white and red wine for drinking straightaway. You might want more whites in summer and more reds in winter.

■ Six special bottles that you intend to keep. Which wines those will be depends on your personal taste and your budget, but it's really only worth keeping high quality dry white wines such as good white Burgundy, or Alsace and German Riesling, high quality or oak-aged reds (claret, Burgundy, Rhône wines or some of the richer, oakier wines from Spain and Portugal) and rich dessert wines like Sauternes.

■ Six 'experiments' or bargains. Maybe the odd bottle that you read about and want to try, or one that you see on special offer.

■ A couple of bottles of sparkling wine – maybe a bottle of Champagne and a more inexpensive sparkler (you could keep one in the fridge).

■ A couple of half bottles of sherry – a dry fino and a nutty amontillado (the fino could also be kept refrigerated).

■ A half bottle of dessert wine like a French Muscat or Sauternes.

■ A good quality bottle of port. Worth buying when you see it at a good price as it will last a good few years unopened.

Storage

You don't have to have a purpose-built space for your wine. A garage or spare bedroom will do, or even the cupboard under the stairs. What is important is that the temperature is reasonably constant.

CHAPTER 24

Finding Out More

Hopefully you will by now be so fired up about wine that you can't wait to learn more about it! There's no shortage of information; there are many excellent books around and most local colleges run some kind of an evening class in wine appreciation. There are also local wine societies in some areas that organise tastings.

Tasting wine is, in fact, by far the best (and the most pleasurable) way to learn about it. Experiment with new wines whenever you can rather than always going for your tried and tested favourites, or even better, set up a tasting with a few friends or colleagues at work.

Organising a tasting

There isn't a lot to organising a tasting but in order to get something out of it, it pays to compare wines of a similar type and price so that you can draw some conclusions about what you like and don't like. For instance, you could compare wines made from the same grape variety in different countries such as Cabernet Sauvignon from France, Bulgaria, Australia, New Zealand, Chile and South Africa. (Keep the number of bottles to around six to eight otherwise the whole exercise can get out of hand!)

If you're trying a number of wines, it's wise to assume some people may want to spit them out (or pour out the remains of the previous wine in their glass) as they go, so provide a couple of large bowls or buckets within easy reach, unless you want disaster to befall your carpet. You also need a wine glass per person (as big a glass as possible so people can get a good sniff of what they're tasting – see Chapter 3), plus an extra glass for water which you should provide on the table. Pens and paper – or if you're feeling really enthusiastic a tasting sheet with each of the wines listed and a space for comments – are handy so you can refer back to your notes at some later point.

Getting a qualification

You can study for a basic qualification in wine on courses approved by the Wine and Spirit Education Trust. Send for a prospectus or contact them at Five Kings House, 1 Queen Street Place, London EC4R 1QS (tel 071 329 0298).

But whether you want to become a serious wine buff or not, the most important thing about wine is to enjoy it. What I hope you'll get from this book is the encouragement to experiment and the self-confidence not to be put off drinking the wines that give you the most pleasure.